"*Leading from the Heart* has challenged me to stoke my fire so that I can minister to my cell members through the power of the Spirit and the fruits that come naturally when I yield control to the Good Shepherd."

Randall G. Neighbour
Editor, Cell Group Journal™

"Michael Mack is one of the early pioneers of the small group movement in the U.S. Whatever he writes, I read. This is one book you won't want to miss because it is far more than just another How To book on small groups. It focuses on the spiritual dimension and goes to the heart of the matter."

Bill Easum
President, Easum, Bandy & Associates

"This book, *Leading from the Heart*, answers three important questions frequently asked by those involved in small groups: 'How do I identify leaders? How do I operate as God's leader? How do I train others to lead?' Mack gives practical illustrations and suggestions in answering these questions. But the unique contribution is that the answers address the heart."

Bill Beckham
President, TOUCH® Global

"In a world of technique and methods, this book takes leadership beyond simply 'doing leadership' to 'becoming a leader after God's own heart.' Mike Mack has not shrunk back from declaring what God wants for you as a small group leader while at the same time authentically sharing from his own heart and wealth of experience. An excellent book for small group leadership teams to go through together."

Dan Lentz
Director, smallgroups.com

Praise for
Leading from the Heart

"Michael Mack approaches leadership in this book like he approaches life . . . from the heart! I believe this is Mike's best work yet. A succinct, clear challenge to lead as Jesus lead."

Thom Corrigan
Decentralization Specialist
Author of Experiencing Community

"Michael Mack has prepared an anointed document that captures the very soul of cell leadership principles. It would be excellent for use in training all cell members and perhaps mandatory for apprentice cell leaders."

Dr. Ralph W. Neighbour, Jr.
Founder, TOUCH® Outreach Ministries

"I have read many books on leadership, both Christian and secular. Almost all of them have been helpful but they are often overwhelming. I found *Leading from the Heart* to be a refreshing change. Instead of simply challenging me to a list of new practices and principles, it invited me to let God renew my heart. Reading this delightful book about the heart of leadership is like drinking from a fresh, cool spring."

Dr. Jim Egli
Small Groups Pastor, Champaign (IL) Vineyard

Leading from the
Heart

Leading from the
Heart

A Group Leader's Guide to a
Passionate Ministry

MICHAEL C. MACK

Cell Group Resources™, a division of TOUCH® Outreach Ministries
Houston, Texas, U.S.A.

Published by Cell Group Resources™
P.O. Box 7847
Houston, Texas, 77270, U.S.A.
800-735-5865

Cover design by Neubauer Design Group, Franklin, TN
Editing by Scott Boren

Library of Congress Cataloging-in-Publication Data

Mack, Michael C., 1960-
    Leading from the heart : a group leader's guide to a passionate
ministry / by Michael C. Mack.
    p. cm.
    Includes biographical references.
    ISBN 1-880828-35-9 (pbk.)
    1. Christian Leadership—Biblical teaching.   2. Leadership in the
Bible.   3. David, King of Israel.   I. Title.
    BS1199.L4 M23 2001
    253—dc21
                                                        2001005022
                                                              CIP

Cell Group Resources™ is a book publishing division
of TOUCH® Outreach Ministries, a resource and consulting ministry
for churches with a vision for missional living through holistic small
groups.

Find us on the World Wide Web at:
http://www.touchusa.org

TO HEIDI,

My wife and best friend. You're in my heart and in my soul.
You are the second best thing to ever happen in my life!

Acknowledgments

In memory of my mom, who taught me about God's heart and has constantly encouraged me to become who God created me to be.

My deep appreciation goes to:

Friends, pastors, and mentors who have trained and discipled me in the ways of heart and soul leadership: Dru Ashwell, Dana Eynon, John Sample, Barbara Bolton, Jim Dahlman, Mark Taylor, Dick Alexander, Glen Elliot, Don Imel, Chris Blair, Bob Bell, Jeffrey Arnold, and Doug Peake.

My cousin and lifelong friend, KC. You have sustained me and influenced my life more than you will ever know.

My accountability partner, Kevin Mitchell. As iron sharpens iron, you've sharpened me and spurred me on. I appreciate you for speaking the truth in love!

The small group leaders and coaches at Foothills Christian Church. It is a blessing to work with people like you who demonstrate such godly hearts.

The small group ministry assistant at Foothills, Carl Douthit. Thanks for your commitment to community life and your help with ideas and reading through this manuscript.

Dan Lentz, director of SmallGroups.com. You are making my dream a reality of providing ongoing training to develop heart and soul small group leadership who are fulfilling Christ's commission.

The great people at TOUCH®: Randall Neighbour, Scott Boren, Don Tillman, and others. It is such a blessing to know you all and work with you.

My wife, Heidi, and my kids, Jordan, Dru, Sarah, and Annie. You inspire me every single day of my life. I am so glad God gave us each other!

And finally, you, the reader. God has chosen you and called you and empowered you as His own child to carry out the family business of reconciling His world for Him. I pray this book will help you live out His purpose for you.

Contents

Foreword

I met Michael Mack nearly ten years ago. At the time, he was an editor of adult curriculum at Standard Publishing.

Right away we hit it off. He was committed to developing small groups in homes for caring and outreach. In fact, he and his wife were leading a recovery group for several people in his own home.

In *Leading from the Heart*, Michael Mack defines the kind of person needed to lead small groups. His emphasis on character development for small group leaders is desperately needed.

I like his idea of using this book for a "turbo" group for training future leaders through a ten-week leadership group. This is an excellent way to give future leaders some "hands on" experience before starting their group.

I also commend TOUCH® Outreach Ministries for offering the church in America a way to plug in the small group ministry in all types of churches, from the traditional church with an established Sunday school program to all types of cutting edge churches using cells as their primary means of evangelism and discipleship.

The small group movement needs a variety of models for assisting the traditional church in the twenty-first century, and this book offers a great contribution in the field. I highly recommend this book.

Lyman Coleman
Author and Founder of Serendipity House

Introduction

He was described simply as "impressive." He was young and tall and without equal among his peers. His dad was a man of standing and substance. Good lineage. He was successful: A hero who rescued an entire city from the enemy. On top of all that, he was chosen by God and empowered by the Spirit. He was made leader of the land. And he seemed so humble about it all. At first, anyway.

After awhile, pride began to sink in, and this seemingly strong leader began to act foolishly and impatiently. Eventually, this led him to disobey a direct order from his main advisor. Then he lied about it and tried to talk his way out of it.

You see, this mighty man had a heart and soul problem. As impressive as he was on the outside, he was weak and sick on the inside. And so God took everything from him and promised it to someone else — someone after His own heart.

The whole story is in 1 Samuel 9-15. The leader in the story is Saul, first King of Israel. He had all of the outward characteristics of a great leader. God chose him based on the people's desires and their ideas of what a great leader would be. But that didn't work. It never had a chance to work. It never will work.

Unfortunately, when we as people look for leaders, we tend to look at what we can discern with our senses: knowledge, skills, personality, ability to communicate, even looks. When we do, we set our churches up for failure. Too many ministries have stalled or crashed because their leaders were selected based on the wrong things. We must look at leadership the way God does. He looks much deeper; He searches a person's heart.

> *When we as people look for leaders, we tend to look at what we can discern with our senses.*

If you are a small group pastor or coach, you need to grasp a clear understanding of this. If you are a group leader, you need to discern what God sees as important about your own leadership. The leader's knowledge, skills, personality, and looks are not as significant as what lies underneath all that: the heart and soul of the person.

After the Lord rejected the leadership of Saul, He set out to establish a king who would have the heart of God. So He sent his prophet Samuel to Bethlehem to anoint one of Jesse's sons as His new leader over Israel. Samuel took one look at the oldest son, Eliab, and thought, *That's the one!* Surely he was the man the Lord would anoint as king. Wrong. Samuel was still looking at things the way the people of Israel had when they desired a leader other than God.

> *The leader's knowledge, skills, personality, and looks are not as significant as what lies underneath all that: the heart and soul of the person.*

Samuel had an important lesson to learn. The Lord told him, "Do not consider his appearance or height, for I have rejected him. The Lord does not look at the things man looks at. Man looks at the outward appearance, but the Lord looks at the heart." Of course, God had already chosen the youngest son, the shepherd, David, "a man after [God's] own heart" (1 Samuel 13:14). And that is the kind of small group leader God seeks: one after His own heart.

How to See the Heart

Jerry was my first intern, and he had great potential: a Bible college degree, the gift of leadership, charisma, a wonderful ability to communicate, and good looks to boot. Only one small problem: He would not make the time or commitment to be an intern. His career and a number of multi-level marketing moonlighting jobs kept him busy all the time. At that stage in his life, he was focused on accumulating money more than anything else, including shepherding our group. He had the outward appearances of a great leader, but at that time in his life, anyway, not the heart.

Since that time, I have learned to look for leaders the way God would — at the heart. That's not as easy. You must get out of the physical domain and into the spiritual realm. The only way of doing this is by following Jesus' directive for finding workers to go into the harvest fields: pray (Matthew 9:37-38)!

Jesus set the example for us when He spent the night in prayer before choosing His twelve interns (Luke 6:12-13). Prayer changes our focus from the outward, physical appearance to the inward, spiritual side of things. It enables us to search the heart.

Jesus was consistent with the Father's nature when He chose the twelve disciples, designating them apostles. Whom did He choose? He did not look at the outward appearance; He looked at the heart and chose smelly fishermen, a suspicious tax collector, and an anti-government zealot. They may not have looked like leaders even three years later when Jesus died but Jesus was able to see something beneath the surface. He saw beyond what they were to what they *could be*. He saw more than smelly fishermen; he saw their potential to become fishers of men.

After Jesus returned to Heaven and these disciples began preaching the gospel on the streets of Jerusalem, two of them were brought before the Jewish leaders and ordered to cease their activities. When these religious leaders "saw the courage of Peter and John and realized they were unschooled, ordinary men, they were astonished and they took note that these men had been with Jesus" (Acts 4:13). Because these Jewish leaders only looked at the outward appearance of these bold, godly, and ragged-looking men, they were astonished at their power. Their boldness and power came from the time they had spent with Jesus. Time spent watching Him do the "impossible." Time spent seeing the way Jesus touched people. Time spent listening to Him pray to the Father. Time spent in hands-on training and involvement, seeing God work through their own lives. Time spent, more than anything else, in relationship with Him as a friend and follower.

> *There is no substitute in a Christian leader's life for time spent in intimate community with Jesus.*

There is no substitute in a Christian leader's life for time spent in intimate community with Jesus. It develops the heart and soul of the leader.

Woe or Go?

Jesus had warned the Jewish leaders about the state of their hearts. They had all of their outward appearances down pat, but their hearts were far from God. " 'Thus you nullify the Word of God for the sake of your tradition,' Jesus told them. 'You hypocrites! Isaiah was right when he prophesied about you, 'These people honor me with their lips, but their hearts are far from me. They worship me in vain. Their teachings are but rules taught by men' " (Matthew 15:6-9).

This was a regular "discussion" Jesus had with the Pharisees and Teachers of the Law. Later, Jesus told them matter-of-factly,

> *Woe to you, teachers of the law and Pharisees, you hypocrites! You are like whitewashed tombs, which look beautiful on the outside but on the inside are full of dead men's bones and everything unclean. In the same way, on the outside you appear to people as righteous but on the inside you are full of hypocrisy and wickedness. (Matthew 23:27-28)*

"Man looks at the outward appearance, but the Lord looks at the heart." Sometimes He doesn't like what He sees! The Pharisees and Teachers of the Law were the "leaders" of their time and culture. Though they knew the Scriptures and undoubtedly had leadership skills, Jesus chose none of them to be his interns. He looked at their wicked hearts and said "woe." But to his disciples He said, "go." As leaders in God's church, we had better be sure that when He looks into *our* hearts, He says "go," and not "woe!"

The Key Question

What of these would you say is the key question for a small group leader?

- Has your group multiplied?
- Are you developing an apprentice leader?
- Are you and your group members sharing your faith?
- Is the group growing in size?
- Has your group done a service project together?
- How are you doing in facilitating discussion in your group?
- How are you shepherding your group?
- How is your own quiet time going?
- How is your relationship with God?

My choice would be the last question. The one before it comes close, but it is only a *result* or *reflection* of the main point. The key question: How is your relationship with God? It gets to the heart of the matter. The other questions are relevant, but the heart question is of paramount importance. *"Above all else, guard your heart, for it is the wellspring of life"* (Proverbs 4:23).

Values

One of the TOUCH® conferences I had the privilege of leading is *Upward, Inward, Outward, Forward.* The four dynamics of a cell or small group (I will use these terms interchangeably in this book) discussed in this workshop are also the guiding values for small group ministry. The essence of this interactive workshop for cell members is that with Christ in our midst we move *Upward* toward God, *Inward* toward each other in body life, *Outward* toward the world in friendship evangelism, and *Forward* toward leadership development in multiplication.

These four dynamics are the heart and soul of a small group; when you as a leader use them as the guiding values for the group, I guarantee fruitfulness! When you allow these values to guide the group, they will free you to become the shepherd, servant, and facilitator you are called to be.

This book is a companion guide to TOUCH's® *Upward, Inward, Outward, Forward Workshop* and *Cell Group Leader Training.* It is written especially for those of you on the front lines of small group leadership: coaches, leaders, interns, and members. My prayer is that it will help you develop the heart and soul of a godly small group leader.

Using This Book

The bookshelves in my church office are packed with "how to" small group books. *Leading from the Heart* has been written to help you, the reader, develop the *internal* qualities a godly, fruit-bearing leader must have.

God's Word provides the pattern for what a small group — and a small group leader — should be. The New Testament especially provides us with many principles for the life of a group. Remember that the Epistles were written to people who were part of house churches in various cities. (See Romans 16:3-5; Philemon 2) Under-standing their context is vital if we are to get a true grasp of the writers' messages to the church. The instructions in these letters (as well as the histories in the Gospels and Acts) were written to people who experienced "church" in small groups!

> *Leading from the Heart has been written to help you, the reader, develop the internal qualities a godly, fruit-bearing leader must have.*

If you are reading an exhortation or instruction for the church, try reading it as possible instructions for your small group. When Paul is discussing the "body of Christ," read it as if it were to the members of your group as well as the whole "congregation."

Consider the following decrees Paul wrote to the church at Colosse. Try reading this passage as instructions to your small group.

> *Bear with each other and forgive whatever grievances you may have against one another. Forgive as the Lord forgave you. And over all these virtues put on love, which binds them all together in perfect unity.*
>
> *Let the peace of Christ rule in your hearts, since as members of one body you were called to peace. And be thankful. Let the word of Christ dwell in you richly as you teach and admonish one another with all wisdom, and as you sing psalms, hymns and spiritual songs with gratitude in your hearts to God. And whatever you do, whether in word or deed, do it all in the name of the Lord Jesus, giving thanks to God the Father through him. (Colossians 3:13-17)*

Ask yourself this: how might these principles affect the life of your group? How would they transform your community if you applied them?

Heart to Heart

The goal of this book is to help leaders apply these biblical truths to their own lives and their groups.

> *The goal of this book is to help leaders apply these Biblical truths to their own lives and their groups.*

This book is designed so that a group leader, coach, or pastor can have individuals read one chapter each week and then use the "Heart to Heart" questions at the end of each chapter in a meeting or one-on-one time to discuss ideas and application.

The "Heart to Heart" questions can be used in a variety of ways. One application is in a training group for new leaders. I have found that one of the best ways to train potential or emerging leaders is to have them experience community together in what I call a "turbo group." For about ten weeks the turbo group meets and models small group life. We start with a barbecue and end with a party; in between, we meet each week and care for one another. Ask these questions during the Word portion of the meeting. You can reference the introductory section about David in each chapter, as well as the corresponding Bible verses or other verses that apply from that chapter. I use the natural, teachable moments that occur in a small group context to train these future leaders in some of the "how to's," of leadership.

Coaches and pastors can also use the "Heart to Heart" times provided to equip current leaders through regular meetings together. This can be done one-on-one or as a group of cell leaders.

Another option is to use this section in a mentoring time with your intern or another potential leader. Read the chapter beforehand, and then meet to discuss it, using the "Heart to Heart" questions. Note that there are just a few open-ended questions per week. Use each question to get a conversation started about the topic. You may spend an hour or more on just a couple questions.

One more thing before we dive right into the heart of the book: I cannot give you the heart and soul of a godly leader through what I have written in the following pages. Only the Holy Spirit brings that kind of inner transformation. The purpose of this book is to walk with you through God's Word to discover His heart and help you apply His truth for you as a shepherd of His flock.

He says to you, leader,

For I know the plans I have for you, plans to prosper you and not to harm you, plans to give you hope and a future. Then you will call upon me and come and pray to me, and I will listen to you. You will seek me and find me when you seek me with all your heart. (Jeremiah 29:11-13)

Chapter One

The Heart of the Father

In order to have the heart *of* the Father, we must begin by having a heart *for* the Father. David had such a heart for God. His extensive writings in the Psalms reveal his passion for knowing God and being known by God. David's delight was "in the law of the Lord," meditating on it day and night (Psalm 1:2). He said that his soul panted and thirsted for God (Psalm 42:1).

He was a godly leader because he sought communion with God. Because he was in relationship with his Creator, he was obedient to Him; this relationship caused him to repent quickly when he wronged God. He desired to seek God's direction for decisions he made. His heart *for* God made him a person who had the heart *of* God. It was that heart that made him a strong and stable leader whose kingdom would last forever and from whose royal lineage would come the Messiah (2 Samuel 7:15-16; Isaiah 9:7).

As a leader of a small group, it is essential to understand God's heart and for His heart to be formed in you. Christian leadership starts with a vital relationship with God. As J. Oswald Sanders said, "Everything in our Christian life and service flows from our relationship with God. If we are not in vital fellowship with Him, everything else will be out of focus."[1]

> *In order to have the heart of the Father, we must begin by having a heart for the Father.*

What Is God's Heart?

The leader's desire should be to have God's heart formed in him. This raises two questions: (1) What is the nature of God's heart, and (2) How does this formation take place?

God's Heart Revealed: He is Relational

When God created mankind, He gave His people a purpose: to rule over His creation (Genesis 1:26-30; 2:15). Then, He chose to have a personal relationship with them. This is an incredible thought to consider. We are not a cosmic mistake. We are more than just pieces of flesh brought into meaningless existence by some uninterested creator. The all-powerful, all-knowing, eternal God made us in His own image and then made us partners with Him in His Creation! And not just business partners, but intimate friends!

After creating Adam, God perceived that the man had a need: "It is not good for the man to be alone." So the Lord provided him with what he needed — a mate — to complete him. In order to show man that He was a God who provides (Jehovah Jireh), God provided the woman for Adam. In so doing, He satisfied Adam's need for companionship and tangibly demonstrated that He cares intimately for his children and that He is a trustworthy provider.

> God has created us for the powerful purpose of showing His love to the world.

God gave no other part of his creation the kind of purpose or relationship He invested in mankind. We are exceedingly special to God. We are created in God's image, the masterpieces of His creation. But we are even more than that; we are His "workmanship" created with an important purpose in His creation. We are "meaningful players in a cosmic drama, intended to know that more is going on beyond what we can see."[2]

God's Heart Revealed:
We Are His Work of Art in Progress

As artists take great pleasure in the works of art they have created, so God takes great pleasure in each one of us. As artists or poets see what they create as an extension of themselves, so God sees us; we are created in His image! And just as artists or artisans do not ultimately create something only for their own enjoyment, but to be enjoyed and used by others, so God has created us for the powerful purpose of showing His love to the world.

Yet we as God's works of art often fail to be the people God had in mind when He created us. We often set our expectations far too low.

I'm amazed how often people tell me, "I don't have any spiritual gifts." I tell them straight out, "Don't say that about God!" They usually look at me with a blank stare and say "huh?" to which I respond, "God is the one who gives us our gifts and enables us to serve Him. When you say you have no gifts or abilities, you're saying more about God than about yourself; you're saying that God hasn't gifted you."

When God called Moses to bring His people out of Egypt, Moses balked. "Who am I to do this?" he asked (Exodus 3:11). God said, "I'll be with you," and Moses replied, "What if it doesn't work out?" Moses fought God's calling with his own deprecation, saying, "I can't do it. I am too slow of speech and tongue." God didn't mince words with Moses: "Who gave man his mouth? ... Is it not I, the Lord? Now go; I will help you speak and will teach you what to say" (Exodus 4:11-12). Still, Moses told God, "Send someone else to do it"! Then, the Scripture says, "the Lord's anger burned against Moses."

Like many of us, Moses failed to see the power God had put inside of him when He called him into His service. God will provide everything that we need to do what He has assigned to us. His appointing comes with His anointing.

We need to accept the potential and power God has been pouring into us from the very beginning of our lives:

> *For you created my inmost being;*
> *you knit me together in my mother's womb.*
> *I praise you because I am fearfully and wonderfully made;*
> *your works are wonderful,*
> *I know that full well.*
> *My frame was not hidden from you*
> *when I was made in the secret place.*
> *When I was woven together in the depths of the earth,*
> *your eyes saw my unformed body.*
> *All the days ordained for me*
> *were written in your book*
> *before one of them came to be. (Psalm 139:13-16)*

We are God's "work of art," but He is not quite finished yet. The objective of spiritual life is transformation. Paul referred to this transformation as Christ being *formed* in us (Galatians 4:19). In the New Testament, the word "formed" was used to describe the creation and growth of an embryo in its mother's womb. So, we as Christians are in a kind of spiritual gestation process. The process started with our being "made alive to God in Christ Jesus"

(Romans 6:11) when we were born again. And it will culminate when we enter the New Jerusalem, when the "dwelling of God is with men and he will live with them," when everything will be made new (Revelation 21:1-5). In the meantime, we "are being transformed into his likeness with ever-increasing glory" (2 Corinthians 3:18).

God wants us to realize that we are works of art in progress, and we as small group leaders, can impart this truth to others. Søren Kierkegaard summed it up best in his prayer: "And now Lord, with your help I shall become myself."

> *God wants us to realize that we are works of art in progress, and we as small group leaders, can impart this truth to others.*

I am fortunate that several people in my life took the time to help me see beyond my circumstances to something better. They were tools used by God to transform me into what He had in mind for me in His plan for my life. Allow me to share my own personal experiences.

School was a chore for me. I was the youngest and smallest kid in kindergarten, and had underdeveloped language skills. My kindergarten teacher was a Chinese nun who herself had not mastered English. My teacher and I understood each other perfectly, but when the year was over, I was not even close to being ready for first grade.

In fifth grade, I had to go to a special class each day for kids with speech problems. I hated being singled out and pulled out of my class to go to the "speech teacher." Then in sixth grade, a doctor discovered I had diabetes, and I missed three weeks of school. When I returned, my friends treated me like I was "different," and my teachers did nothing to help educate my classmates about the disease.

I struggled academically and socially until eighth grade when two important events changed the direction of my life. The first happened at home. My mom owned and operated a custom drapery shop in the basement of our home. She employed about four women in the shop, all of who became like extended family to me.

One day, out of the blue, in front of everyone, Mom said, "You know, Mike is a really good problem solver. He always uses his creativity to come up with good solutions to difficult situations. He really has a creative mind." It may not seem like much, but her words of encouragement and love still bless me to this day.

The second transformational event in my life happened in my algebra class. I struggled most with math. I had a Chinese teacher, Mrs. Li, who knew very little English. We were moving through the textbook at a snail's pace and learning very little since Mrs. Li was struggling to communicate as well as teach.

About a month into the school year, two of my friends, Paul Augustine and Dale Trebor, went to Mrs. Li and suggested they do an independent study through the math book. She agreed, and with her permission, they asked me to join them. Each day we worked through the textbook by ourselves. If we came across something we didn't understand, we tried to work it out ourselves, and if we really had trouble, we asked Mrs. Li for help. When one of us got stuck on a concept, the other two stopped to help him figure it out. None of us moved on until all three of us got it.

When we finished one textbook, Mrs. Li gave another and let us advance. At the end of the year, Paul, Dale, and I had worked our way through three and a half textbooks! The rest of the class had not even finished the first book.

If you were to ask my friends and co-workers for a reference on me today, they might say a couple positive things about me. First, I'm a creative, big-picture thinker. I'm good at seeing a problem and coming up with creative solutions. Secondly, I'm pretty good with numbers. After my "small group" experience in eighth grade, I went to a private college-prep high school and tutored other kids in algebra.

You see, I was given a *vision* of what I could be, indeed, in what I truly was. I am not the short kid with speech and math problems. God worked through those painful times in my life to develop something inside me that only He could bring about. And, in His design, He used others to show me His plan for my life.

My mom used encouraging words to bring out something good in me, something good that God had created in me. She saw it, helped me to see it, and then helped me become it. She was God's instrument in His process of *transforming* my life.

Paul and Dale included me in their community with a purpose. I believe this was my first small group experience! Together, we spurred each other on and in the process, we connected with each other. We challenged one another and were patient with each other as we moved *together* to become something better.

> Small group leaders have a special privilege of helping people see, understand, and live out the purpose God has created within them.

God has created every person as a unique work of art. His plan is for us to realize this and live it out. But we do not always see the beauty and purpose within us. Small group leaders have a special privilege of helping people see, understand, and live out the purpose God has created within them. It is God's plan to use His people to encourage one another and spur one another on.

God's Heart Revealed: Mercy

God's heart is a heart of mercy. If man had never sinned, this characteristic of God would have remained latent (Romans 11:32). But because mankind did and does sin, God has shown us His great mercy. Throughout Scripture we see His heart of mercy (Exodus 33:19; Psalm 28:6; Daniel 9:18; Micah 7:18; Hosea 6:6; Ephesians 2:4).

> *If we as leaders are to be people after God's own heart, we must be people of mercy.*

David experienced God's mercy firsthand, and as a result he became a person who extended mercy to others; Saul and Mephibosheth are but two examples. That's another reason David was a man after God's own heart.

If we as leaders are to be people after God's own heart, we must be people of mercy:

He has showed you, O man, what is good. And what does the Lord require of you? To act justly and to show mercy and to walk humbly with your God. (Micah 6:8)

God's Heart Revealed: Joy and Celebration

Joy and celebration are at the center of God's heart and character. King David instructed all God's people 102 times in the psalms to "shout for joy," "sing for joy," "leap with joy," "call forth songs of joy," "rejoice in the Lord and be glad." Joy is a central theme throughout the Bible. There are some 448 occurrences of the words *joy, joyous, joyful, rejoice,* and *enjoy* in the NIV. In the Old Testament, God's people were commanded to celebrate at numerous feasts.

In the New Testament, Jesus brought "joy to the world," as the Christmas hymn reminds us. At His birth announcement to the shepherds, the angel said, "Do not be afraid. I bring you good news of great joy that will be for all the people. Today in the town of David a Savior has been born to you; he is Christ the Lord" (Luke 2:10-11).

The Christian life is to be a joy-filled life. That joy is not contingent upon our circumstances. In fact, just the opposite is true. Jesus told his followers that when people hated, excluded, insulted, and rejected them that they should "rejoice in that day and leap for joy" (Luke 6:22-23). James began his letter to encourage Christians the same way: "Consider it pure joy, my brothers, whenever you face trials of many kinds" (James 1:2). The real question is, how do you live this way in the real world?

Rejoice in the Lord always. I will say it again: Rejoice! . . . Do not be anxious about anything, but in everything, by prayer and petition, with thanksgiving, present your requests to God. . . . I have learned to be content whatever the circumstances. I know what it is to be in need, and I know what it is to have plenty. I have learned the secret of being content in any and every situation, whether well fed or hungry, whether living in plenty or in want. I can do everything through him who gives me strength. (Philippians 4:4-13)

I have heard it said that happiness is a choice. In other words, regardless of circumstances, you can choose to be either happy or bitter. That is true to a certain extent, but *joy* is not something we can just put on like a shirt. It is a gift we must receive; it is a fruit of the Spirit (Galatians 5:22). Jesus told his disciples that if they would obey His commands and remain in His love, then His joy would be in them and their joy would be complete (John 15:9-11). Jesus is our joy-giver, and no one can take His joy away from us (John 16:22).

To me, there is nothing more joyful than ministry, especially seeing people become followers of Jesus. Baptisms make me want to dance and shout! But there are many other things in my life that bring joy. My wife and children bring me joy every day. Riding my bike in the mountains brings me a rush of joy as I commune with God in His creation. For me, *living life* is joyful.

The Pharisees in Jesus' day did not know or experience this joy. How could they? They did not know Jesus in their hearts. They lived by a strict set of rules, which weighed them down and brought them no joy. They missed the point of life. They could not understand how Jesus and his disciples could exude such joy and celebration all of the time. Jesus got the reputation of being a glutton and a drunkard because he came eating and drinking rather than fasting and abstaining (Matthew 11:19). He enjoyed a good celebration!

The antagonistic Pharisees were not the only ones who could not comprehend Jesus' joyful lifestyle. Even John the Baptist's disciples came to ask Jesus why He and His disciples did not fast. His response was, basically, "Now is not the time for mourning. While I am with you, it's time to celebrate!"

As a small group leader, I want to be a man after God's own heart and have a joy, joy, joy, joy down in my heart. I want my small group meetings to be celebrations of God's goodness. Joy draws unreached people to God's people and therefore to God.

Laughter is one of the best ways to bring joy into a group. Humor can help people learn. It breaks down defenses we build up toward hard truths. Also, laughter can help facilitate self-disclosure. When people laugh together, they can share more openly together. Laughter breaks down the walls we build around ourselves. It can help people release their pent-up emotions in a positive way. A good belly laugh just feels good, especially when it lets you forget about yourself and your troubles for a while.

You don't have to be a comedian to bring humor into your group. It helps if you show the rest of your group that laughter and joy are acceptable though. Unfortunately, some people think the church is no place to laugh; perhaps they need to read Ecclesiastes again: "There is a time for everything, and a season for every activity under heaven: . . . a time to weep and a time to laugh" (3:1-4). Maybe you can study passages that reveal the humor of Jesus or the apostle Paul. Be willing to laugh at yourself and demonstrate a light-hearted attitude when appropriate.

> *When people laugh together, they can share more openly together.*

Here are a few cautions about using humor in a group. First of all, avoid humor that is in bad taste. Humor does not mean giving up our integrity as Christians. So no racist, sexist, or irreverent jokes, and no jokes at someone else's expense (whether the person is in the group or not). "Nor should there be obscenity, foolish talk or coarse joking, which are out of place" (Ephesians 5:4). Be sure that humor is not deliberately exclusive. A joke or story that is understood by a specific few can do more harm than good. Also, don't try too hard to be funny. Humor should be natural and relaxed, not forced.

One final thing: there is a time for laughter in your group, but not all the time. There are also times for serious discussions and somber emotions. Remember that laughter, like any medicine, is dangerous if you overdose.

History-sharing icebreakers can be a great way to bring joy into the group. For instance, ask everyone to bring a photo of him or herself in elementary or high school. Pictures of out-of-date clothes and hair-styles might be enough to get them laughing, and friendly stories about their childhood or teen years can keep them chuckling. Ask members to share one of the funniest things that has ever happened to them. Ask couples how they met or what humorous things happened while they were dating. From time to time, ask the group to draw pictures, play a silly game together, or do a skit of a Bible story. Use your imagination!

Groups that are becoming close friends with one another, sharing life together, and learning to love one another, will be joyful groups. But joy will spill out of groups that are reaching out and inviting others into the joy-filled life that one can only experience in Jesus Christ. Seeing friends and neighbors and co-workers giving their lives to Jesus brings real joy to any group!

God's Heart Revealed: He Is Love

"God is love" (1 John 4:8 and 16). There is no other attribute of God stated so succinctly in Scripture. Yet our view of God is sometimes distorted. We see Him as a strict judge who wants to condemn us. For example, when I was about five years old, my mom let me play in the front yard . . . with boundaries: I could not step out of the yard or into the driveway. Like most children, I wanted to test my mother's boundaries, so I stepped off the sidewalk step onto the driveway . . . and fell, scraping my knee. As Mom bandaged my knee, she said, "See, God was watching you and made you fall for disobeying me." My mom's intentions were not bad, but I grew up thinking of God as a cosmic policeman just waiting for me to make a mistake so that He could make me fall.

Larry Crabb discusses the fact that we need to view God differently than perhaps we have been programmed to think of Him. Above all else, we need to see His loving kindness and mercy. He says,

> Until we thrill in the Father's embrace after admitting we've been prostitutes, until we watch him jump up and down with delight every time he sees us, until we hear him ask, "How can I help?" when we expected him to say, "I'm sick and tired of putting up with you!" we will not change, not really, not consistently, not deeply.

> Do we see the good in people, the good heart buried beneath all the pettiness and resentments and empire-building ambitions that irritate us so badly? . . .

> Without this foundational element of offering others a taste of Christ's delight in them, all our skillful techniques, our wise counsel, our insightful interpretations, even our warm encouragement, will add up to nothing.[3]

Changing our perception about God should also lead us to change our perceptions about ourselves and the people around us. As Crabb points out, we need to alter our belief that God's message is, "You're that bad, and don't you forget it!" to "I'm that good. I still like you. I'm for you."[4] God's great, unconditional love for us is the basis for our heart attitudes as leaders. If we are leading for any other reason than love, we are leading for the wrong reason.

"Be on your guard," leader, "against the yeast of the Pharisees, which is hypocrisy" (Luke 12:1). Jesus turned to speak to his disciples after blasting the Pharisees and experts in the law for focusing on outward appearances rather than the inward conditions of their hearts (Luke 11:37-52). They served out of a desire to be seen as holy rather than out of a pure love for others (Luke 11:39-41). Leader, search your heart and examine your motives for serving. If you are leading a group to make yourself look good in front of others, to make you appear spiritual or important or powerful, or to show off your knowledge or leadership skills or personality, then I seriously urge you to reconsider your commitment. Either stop leading or get right with God and let Him change your heart. Repent — change the direction of your service — toward being a person after God's own heart. (This is a continuous process in life, not a one-time event.) *Then* lead out of the overflow of your heart ... God's heart of unconditional love.

> *If we are leading for any other reason than love, we are leading for the wrong reason.*

Let me encourage you, leader: "Above all else, guard your heart, for it is the wellspring of life" (Proverbs 4:23).

Life to the Full

A man once came across an accident where a woman was bending over and attending to one of the victims. The man rushed over, shoved the woman aside, and said, "Here, let me at him. I've had a course in first aid."

The woman stepped back and said, "Well, when you get to the part in your course where it says, 'Call a doctor,' I'll be right here."

How often do we do that with God?

All too often, we, as leaders in the church, act — and live — like we don't really need God. I love the way one of my seminary professors put it:

> The voice of Jesus saying, "*I* will build my church" can hardly be heard among the babble of human voices saying, "*We* will build the church. Our plans, our organizations, our resources will accomplish it, and we will have it the way we want it." God is sometimes boxed out of His own enterprise by self-centered or self-sufficient partners.[5]

The longer I'm a Christian, the more I understand that, as a leader, my relationship with God is the most important thing in my life. It has taken a lot of painful lessons to realize that I do not have to be "the man" in order to make things happen in ministry. When I tried to do everything I thought I needed to do to make my ministry successful, I learned quickly and painfully that I couldn't do it, and I felt guilty for not doing it all. Then I came across the words of Jesus in His prayer in John 17: "I have brought you glory on earth by completing the work you gave me to do" (John 17:4). Did Jesus heal every sick person? Did He preach the gospel to every single living being at that time? No, but He *did* accomplish what the Father had given Him to do. And that is what I want to happen in my ministry. I know that I am accountable to God to do what He has called me to do today. Little things, even interruptions from my schedule, are opportunities from God. *He* is the Lord of my life, not my "to do" list!

I have had to learn to discern between activity *for* God and the activity *of* God. I can't say this has been easy. Sometimes I just have to stop and rest from *my* work for a while and trust in *His* work in me. I have to watch how I view people: do I love them for what they can do for me, or do I simply love them for who they are?

As a small group leader, I can't do everything for everyone all the time. I have to remember that the group belongs to God, not to me. At the same time, I am a steward of these people God has given me, so I must take that responsibility seriously. Later in His prayer in John 17, Jesus said, "I have revealed you to those whom you gave me out of the world. They were yours; you gave them to me and they have obeyed your word" (John 17:6). Like Jesus, God has entrusted us as stewards with the people in our groups.

The role of a group leader is not to create a codependent relationship with the group. It is to serve them, love them, grow them, and release them to do the work of ministry in the group. God has blessed us with a huge responsibility; at the same time, we must understand that we are simply the tools God uses to accomplish His will.

Once, John Wesley reportedly received a note from a self-appointed evangelist saying, "The Lord has told me to tell you that He doesn't need your book learning, your Greek and Hebrew." Wesley replied bluntly, "Thank you, sir. Your letter was superfluous, however, as I

> *All too often, we act like we don't really need God.*

already knew the Lord has no need of my book learning, as you put it. However, although the Lord has not told me to say so, on my own responsibility I would like to say to you that the Lord does not need your ignorance either."

The Lord doesn't really *need* our efforts, does He? However, "[God] has committed to us the message of reconciliation. We are therefore Christ's ambassadors, as though God were making his appeal through us" (2 Corinthians 5:19-20). God has chosen to use us as His representatives. But the power comes from Him, not from us.

Ask yourself these questions: Are you experiencing God and the fullness that comes from Him? Do you have life and have it to the full?

If you want to go deeper into the fullness of God, I want to challenge you to do four things:

1. Make it a priority to nurture your relationship with God through *personal* Bible study, prayer, and worship because God wants to know you and be known by you.

2. Find an accountability or support partner. Talk several times a week and encourage one another to continue the search for intimacy with God.

3. Don't forsake your relationships with your family, your group, or your church. Draw upon the relationship you are developing with God and be a godly influence on those around you. God yearns not only for us to have communion with Him, but also for us to be in community with one another.

4. Do what Jesus did. Get away from the crowds, and even your small group, every once in a while. Simply commune with the Father: come into His presence, find rest, and draw closer to His heart.

Jesus promised life to the full to everyone who follows Him. When He is truly Lord of every part of your life, and you seek His will, not your own, then you will have that life. How does this happen in practice? Model your life after Jesus and the way He followed God in His earthly ministry.

As you read the next chapter, take time to write out your own specific plan for living your life and leading your group by Jesus' pattern.

Heart to Heart

1. What does being a person after God's own heart look like in real life? Describe such a person.

2. As you look through the attributes of God's heart, in which areas are you already strong? Where do you personally need to be transformed to become a more Godly person?

3. How do you become a leader after God's own heart? On a day-to-day basis, what will you do to be transformed into such a leader?

4. At the end of the chapter, we were challenged to do four things. Let's discuss these and write out plans to make them part of our lives.

Chapter Two

The Heart of Jesus

One of Jesus' names was "The Son of David." God ordained that the Messiah would come through the lineage of David, the man after God's own heart. The Son of David was simply an earthly title for the Son of God who was not only a man *after* God's heart, but also one whose heart was the exact representation of His Father's. He said about himself, "Anyone who has seen me has seen the Father" (John 14:9).

I love it when someone says about one of my four children, "He or she is the spittin' image of you!" (when they mean it as a compliment)! "Jordan has your creativity." "Dru is athletic like you." "Sarah's compassion is just like yours." "Annie must have caught her energy and focus from you!" Somehow, from genetics or upbringing or both, each one of my children has a part of my heart. Just as I am pleased with my children when they reflect what is good in my heart, so God was "well pleased" with His Son, Jesus (Matthew 3:17; 17:5).

When you look at Jesus in the Gospels, you get a view of the heart of God that we as humans can relate to. As we watch Him dealing with different kinds of people, making disciples, and leading His small group, we get a glimpse of God's heart in human settings. Matthew 9 and 10 show at least six aspects of Jesus' heart that all Christian leaders should model. Please read the following passage and various aspects of it will be discussed through the rest of this chapter.

> *As we watch Jesus dealing with different kinds of people, we get a glimpse of God's heart in human settings.*

As Jesus went on from there, he saw a man named Matthew sitting at the tax collector's booth. "Follow me," he told him, and Matthew got up and followed him. While Jesus was having dinner at Matthew's house, many tax collectors and "sinners" came and ate with him and his disciples. When the Pharisees saw this, they asked his disciples, "Why does your teacher eat with tax collectors and 'sinners'?" On hearing this, Jesus said, "It is not the healthy who need a doctor, but the sick. But go and learn what this means: 'I desire mercy, not sacrifice.' For I have not come to call the righteous, but sinners." (Matthew 9:9-13

Jesus went through all the towns and villages, teaching in their synagogues, preaching the good news of the kingdom and healing every disease and sickness. When he saw the crowds, he had compassion on them, because they were harassed and helpless, like sheep without a shepherd. Then he said to his disciples, "The harvest is plentiful but the workers are few. Ask the Lord of the harvest, therefore, to send out workers into his harvest field." He called his twelve disciples to him and gave them authority to drive out evil spirits and to heal every disease and sickness. (Matthew 9:35-10:1)

To be godly leaders like Jesus, we need to develop an authentic heart, a servant's heart, a compassionate heart, a shepherd's heart, a heart connected to God, and a disciple-making heart.

An Authentic Heart

Jesus was the most authentic leader who ever lived. He was real. He wore no masks to hide his true identity. He was transparent.

An inauthentic leader never would have picked Matthew as one of his disciples. He would not even have stopped to talk with him at his tax collector's booth. Tax collectors like Matthew were hired by the hated Romans to collect taxes from their fellow Jews, and usually extorted money from them. But Jesus saw the person Matthew *really* was, instead of only seeing his profession.

An inauthentic leader would have avoided having dinner at Matthew's house with a bunch of other tax collectors and "sinners" because of appearances if nothing else. "Bad company corrupts good character," the Greek saying went.[1] Or, as my mom used to put it when she wasn't too sure of the friends I was picking, "Show me who you're going with, and I'll show you who you are."

> *Jesus was the most authentic leader who ever lived.*

The Pharisees, whom we have already discussed as being inauthentic leaders, showed up at the party too. They came not to join in the festivities, but to take the opportunity to cast judgment on Jesus and His followers.

Jesus stood up to the inauthentic Pharisees: People who are sick need doctors, not people who are healthy. I came to save sinners, not to have theological discussions with those who already think they are righteous! (cf. Matthew 9:12).

Jesus was the perfect example of a *real* leader, one who illustrated Paul's instructions: "Do not be proud, but be willing to associate with people of low position" (Romans 12:16). An authentic leader is concerned with serving God, not pleasing men (Galatians 1:10; 1 Thessalonians 2:4). If you are given a trust to shepherd God's people in a small group, or any other ministry, your concern is proving faithful to God rather than winning the approval of men (see 1 Corinthians 4:1-5).

Part of Jesus' authenticity was His transparency. He feasted and laughed with those who were joyful; He cried with those who mourned; He got angry with those who exploited others and God. Jesus never hid behind a mask.

As a small group leader, you must have that kind of authenticity. You must lead in transparency and vulnerability. You have to open up your life before your group members will do the same. Transparency about little things at first will enable people to be open about bigger things later.

> *As a small group leader, you must lead in transparency and vulnerability.*

One of the most transparent leaders I've ever known is my friend Kevin. One week as he led our couples group, he made an offhand comment about his wife, Ginger. Kevin didn't realize he had just insulted his wife, but the rest of the group saw the expression on Ginger's face. The next week, Kevin brought Ginger in front of the group and apologized to her publicly, and then he apologized to the rest of the group as well. His vulnerability modeled for the rest of us how a husband *should* treat his wife and how a Godly leader can lead by example.

A Servant's Heart

Many of us have been told that, as Christian leaders, we are to be *servant-leaders*. But what exactly does that mean? Isn't the idea of being a *servant-leader* a paradox? If not, what does *servant-leadership* look like?

Our best example of servant-leadership is Jesus. He came to earth to take the very nature of a servant (Philippians 2:6-7). He modeled that attitude throughout His life. After calling Matthew to follow Him, Jesus healed a dead girl, a sick woman, a blind man, and a mute, demon-possessed man. Matthew 9:35 summarizes Jesus' ministry: "Jesus went through all the towns and villages, teaching in their synagogues, preaching the good news of the kingdom and healing every disease and sickness." He came not to be served, but to serve. Jesus exemplified servant-leadership.

Still, His followers didn't "get it." One time, James and John asked Jesus for a favor: "Let us have the best seats in your kingdom." That upset the rest of the disciples, who apparently didn't want to be left out. Jesus responded firmly,

You know that the rulers of the Gentiles lord it over them, and their high officials exercise authority over them. Not so with you. Instead, whoever wants to become great among you must be your servant, and whoever wants to be first must be your slave — just as the Son of Man did not come to be served, but to serve, and to give his life as a ransom for many. (Matthew 20:25-28)

On another occasion, the disciples actually argued over who was the greatest (Luke 9:46). Jesus used a little child to show them what kind of leader He wanted them to be saying, "For he who is least among you all — he is the greatest" (Luke 9:48).

There are basically two kinds of leaders: those who focus on being the "greatest," that is, "leaders first," and those who focus on being the "least," that is, "servants first." In the following chart is a list of differences between these two kinds of leaders:[2]

LEADERS FIRST	SERVANTS FIRST
Naturally tries to control, make decisions, and give orders.	Assumes leadership only if it is the best way to serve.
"Driven" to lead.	"Called" to lead.
Possessive about leadership position — they think they "own" it.	Views leadership as an act of stewardship rather than ownership. If someone else is a better leader, they will partner with the person or find another place to serve.
Dislikes feedback — it is threatening to their position.	Likes feedback — it helps them serve better.

Paul, James, Peter, Jude, and John were all servants first. They begin their letters by referring to themselves first as servants, and then as leaders (Romans 1:1; James 1:1; 2 Peter 1:1; Jude 1; Revelation 1:1).

A servant's heart is critical to spiritual leadership. As the small group leader, seek first to serve the people in your group. Spend time with them outside of meetings, and learn how to meet their needs. Pray for each one regularly (daily, if you really mean it!). Model the New Testament "one anothers" to the group and call them to serve one another in love.

> *There are basically two kinds of leaders: those who focus on being the "greatest," that is, "leaders first," and those who focus on being the "least," that is, "servants first."*

A group I co-led decided to study and practice some of the "one anothers," so I gave each member a list of all the passages that use the words "one another" or "each other" in the New Testament. We met at a different member's home each week; the hosts chose one of the "one another" passages and how to teach and apply it practically. We served one another by washing each other's cars; spoke to one another with psalms, hymns and spiritual songs with an evening of worship using bongos, tambourines, maracas, and all kinds of other fun instruments; spurred each other on by taking turns being encouraged; and, of course, offered hospitality to one another with lots of food and fun! Through these practical lessons, we learned to become a group that loved and cared for each other naturally.

A Compassionate Heart

When Jesus saw the crowds of people who had come to hear him teach and be healed, "he had compassion on them, because they were harassed and helpless, like sheep without a shepherd" (Matthew 9:36).

In the New Testament, when Jesus is "moved to compassion," the word usually refers to a turning point in a person or group's life. When a leper came to Jesus begging for healing, Jesus, "filled with compassion," reached out to touch and heal (Mark 1:40-42).

This same active aspect of compassion is illustrated in two parables Jesus told. In Matthew 18, Jesus told the story of a servant who owed an unpayable debt. He begged the king to whom he was in debt to give him time to repay it. The king was so moved by *compassion* that he cancelled the debt. Luke 15 tells the story of the prodigal son who returned home to confess his sins and beg for a job as a hired hand. The father was "filled with compassion for him" and welcomed him back as a son.

Imagine Jesus walking down the main street of your city today. How do you think He would see people? How would He feel? How would He act? I am certain His heart would be broken, and He would have deep compassion for them. We see business suits and success. I think Jesus would see through the suits and see people who are harassed and helpless, like sheep without a shepherd.

What would happen in Christ's church and today's society if we saw people the way that Jesus sees them? I believe that that *in*sight alone would bring revival! To have the compassion that Jesus had, we need to see their true spiritual condition: lost! The harvest of lost people is still plentiful. It is still the workers that are too few.

> *What would happen in Christ's church and today's society if we saw people the way that Jesus sees them?*

Jesus' compassion led to prayer and service. A small group leader, by definition is someone who has compassion for (1) the people in his group and (2) people outside the group and especially those outside of a relationship with Christ. That compassion lives itself out in action — in meaningful service to and with those people. Service without compassion is meaningless, and compassion is not possible without an ability to see people's true condition. It takes a leader led by the Holy Spirit to have the kind of *in*sight that leads to compassion and prayerful service.

A Shepherd's Heart

Throughout the Old Testament, God is described as a shepherd (e.g. Genesis 48:15; 49:24). "The Lord is my shepherd, I shall not be in want," begins Psalm 23. God chose a shepherd — a man after His own heart — to lead His people (2 Samuel 5:2).

Church leaders are reminded to be shepherds of God's flock, which Jesus bought with His blood (Acts 20:28; 1 Peter 5:2). Small group leaders are actually undershepherds who serve Jesus, the Head Shepherd. They guide people out of compassion as they see the needs of the people around them. Because people are "like sheep without a shepherd," undershepherds step in to represent the Good Shepherd.

Undershepherds — that is, shepherding small group leaders who rely on the power of the Holy Spirit — can see with Jesus' eyes. By Jesus' authority, they become the undershepherd for harassed and helpless sheep. The heart of a shepherd is to "believe in what others can become because they believe the good that exists deep within every regenerate heart is potentially stronger than all the bad that is there."[3] This means that the undershepherd must connect intimately with people in the group, just as the Good Shepherd connects in intimate relationship with us. These shepherds "accept the challenge to identify, nourish, and release the life of God in others by connecting with them."[4]

It is important to make a distinction between serving people as a hired hand and true biblical shepherding. Undershepherds primarily serve *Jesus*, not people. They represent the Good Shepherd as His ambassadors; they are His tools, the workers *He* sends into the harvest field. Whatever they do, they work at it with all their hearts, as serving the Lord, not men (Colossians 3:23). Hired hands often focus their energy serving people before they focus on serving Jesus.

> *Small group leaders are actually undershepherds who serve Jesus, the Head Shepherd.*

When leaders focus wholly on serving *people*, they tend to serve only people's wants and desires. When they primarily serve Jesus, they serve *real* needs and concerns. People's self-perceived needs are often in conflict with what God intends for their lives. One author said, "The servant of Christ is dedicated to making people do what they do not want to do so they can become what they always wanted to be."[5] The danger of serving "people" and their desires is that instead of making true, fully devoted, obedient and active disciples of Christ, what is produced are unhealthy, passive church attendees.

Shepherding people is a lifestyle, not a job or a role we play. That's why shepherding is a matter of the *heart and soul*, not just work we do or service we provide. In John 10:11-15, Jesus contrasted the true shepherd (the Good Shepherd) with a hired hand. In TOUCH's® *Cell Leader and Intern Seminar*, the following chart is used to show the differences:

SHEPHERD	HIRED HAND
Cares to the point of sacrifice.	Quits when it gets tough.
Knows sheep personally.	Knows sheep as a flock.
Intimate relationship to God.	In it for personal advancement.
Heart for the sheep.	Just doing the job.

One other big difference, which will be discussed more in chapter 4 of this book, is that shepherd leaders are *called* or *anointed*, and not just recruited as most hired hands are. Like David, when God calls you to lead, you can be assured that He sees something good in your heart. When God calls you to His service, He provides every resource you will need to accomplish the tasks He gives you. When you enter leadership without God's anointing, you may have to provide your own resources. God loves you and wants the best for your life. He has created you for an intimate relationship with you and a purpose in His kingdom. With this in mind, why in the world would anyone want to step into leadership without God's calling?

The shepherd leader is concerned not only for the sheep in the fold, but also for the lost sheep; Jesus poignantly illustrated this in the parable of the lost sheep (Luke 15:1-7). Once again, Jesus was in the position of defending His actions to the Pharisees, who muttered, "This man welcomes sinners and eats with them." Jesus replied by telling the parable in which the shepherd leaves the ninety-nine safe sheep to find the one lost sheep. He followed up this parable with two more that illustrated the same truth. Three parables, back-to-back, about the importance of finding that which is lost — but the hard-hearted Pharisees still didn't get it. Jesus said, through parable and directly, that he came to save the lost — those who are harassed and helpless, those who were missing a relationship with the Good Shepherd.

> *People's self-perceived needs are often in conflict with what God intends for their lives.*

It is still the same today. Like Jesus, we have been called to go to those in need of a relationship with God, not to stay in the comfy confines of our pews. I've often heard small group leaders say something like, "I'm a shepherding leader, not an evangelistic leader." Entire groups will proclaim, "We're a shepherding group, not an evangelistic group."

> *This is what the Sovereign Lord says: Woe to the shepherds of Israel who only take care of themselves! Should not shepherds take care of the flock? . . . You have not strengthened the weak or healed the sick or bound up the injured. You have not brought back the strays or searched for the lost. . . . My sheep wandered over all the mountains and on every high hill. They were scattered over the whole earth, and no one searched or looked for them. (Ezekiel 34:2-6)*

From this passage, it is clear that part of the job of a shepherd is taking care of the flock. But seeking the lost is equally important. Shepherding and evangelism are not competing or contrasting values. Seeking the lost is *part of* shepherding. Shepherding leaders must have a heart for the lost sheep in their spheres of influence. They must have a heart for helping group members reach out to their lost friends, neighbors, family members, and co-workers.

Shepherd leaders are undershepherds of the Good Shepherd. They have a God-given compassion for people and seek to care for and serve them by Jesus' power. As stated before, they can do none of this in their own strength, but only through the strength God provides.

A Heart Connected to God

My compassion for people typically leads me to *do* something about the situations I see around me. I'm a man of action, and I usually feel pretty good about that. It's the American way. When the going gets tough, the tough get going. In fact, I am sometimes prone to believe, it's not just the American way, it's the Christian way. As I look at how Jesus reacted to situations, I see something different.

His compassion for the harassed and helpless led Him to say to the disciples, "The harvest is plentiful but the workers are few. Ask the Lord of the harvest, therefore, to send out workers into his harvest field."

Let me call attention to what Jesus did *not* say. He didn't say, "The harvest is plentiful but the tithers are few." He didn't say, "The harvest is plentiful but the building costs are too high." He didn't say, "The harvest is plentiful but first we need to start the latest program." No, the problem isn't something we can solve by our own means, ideas, or insights; it is the *workers* who are missing.

> Like Jesus, we have been called to go to those in need of a relationship with God, not to stay in the comfy confines of our pews.

So, where do we find workers? Bible colleges? Seminaries? Parachurch ministries? The Harvard School of Business? No, Jesus said we should ask the Lord of the Harvest, for only He can supply *the workers!* We should go first to our knees and ask God to supply the need. After all, it is *His* harvest field and *His* work.

Jesus made it clear to His followers that He did and said nothing on His own, but only what the Father gave Him to do and say.[6] In the same way, we can do nothing of any value on our own. "No branch can bear fruit by itself; it must remain in the vine. Neither can you bear fruit unless you remain in me. … Apart from me you can do nothing" (John 15:4-5).

Before Jesus took action or asked others to take action, He modeled the most valuable lesson — to take the situation to the only one who is in control. An undershepherd has by definition an intimate relationship with God. That was true of David and Jesus and must be true of us as well.

When I was called to a traditional church in central Indiana to start a small group ministry, I wondered where to look for our future small group leaders. I wanted to start the ministry with a *team* of people. But who? This was a church that had never had a successful small group ministry, so I had no idea where people with the right mindset would come from. I believed that small groups could be the harvest fields where lost people could be found, so it also occurred to me that the Lord of those harvest fields could and would supply the workers. All I had to do was ask.

Even before my first day in the office, I spent time praying over Matthew 9:35-38, asking God to supply workers for the harvest. Soon after moving to town, I met the Morfords and the Smiths, who told me they had been praying and waiting for someone to come to help them start small groups in the church. Both families had been involved in small groups at other churches. God had supplied the first leaders and members of the team. I shared Matthew 9:35-38 with them, and we all began to pray. Soon we came to know the Kellys, who had moved from Virginia, and the Westons, from California. Both families shared incredible stories of how God brought them to our city and church. They joined the team and eventually became small group leaders as well.

> *Before Jesus took action or asked others to take action, He modeled the most valuable lesson ... to take the situation to the only one who is in control.*

God is sovereign over His kingdom and His church. Jesus has promised that *He* would build His church and that the gates of Hell would not prevail against it. He brought workers into His harvest fields in a small town in central Indiana. "Ask the Lord of the harvest, therefore"!

A Disciple Making Heart

What Jesus did after teaching His followers to pray for workers might be a bit surprising to us in the modern church. Jesus called His twelve leaders-in-training to Himself, gave them authority, and sent them out to spread the gospel (Matthew 10:1, ff). What is so amazing is that these men had just been harvested themselves! He sent them right back into the harvest fields as workers doing what Jesus had modeled for them.

The author of this gospel, Matthew, had left behind his accounting books and piles of money to follow Jesus (9:9). Then he threw a dinner party for his friends and invited Jesus and his disciples. He found an opportunity to bring his friends into contact with their Savior. Now, just a chapter later, Matthew is heading out to share the gospel with others.

Matthew may not have had a seminary degree or an abundant knowledge of the Scriptures, but he had a passion for Christ and compassion for the lost. As Neil Cole said, "I'll take a hot, impassioned witness over a cold, knowledgeable one every time."[7] Like Matthew, you and I have been redeemed from our pasts for God's purpose. Why not be like Matthew, who saw his redeemed life as an opportunity to make a difference in his sphere of influence? You are here for a purpose; otherwise God would have already brought you home to Him. Your life is not your own. It was bought at a price, and God has a plan for it.

As a leader with a disciple-making heart, you can help your group reach the lost. Model compassion for the lost; make friendship evangelism a priority in your life. If you don't have any lost friends, make some! Find ways to serve your friends who do not know Jesus. Eat lunch with non-Christian co-workers. Get involved in an activity that gets you interacting with others. Throw a block party. As you develop relationships and then start sharing your faith with others, talk about it with your group, not to brag, but to model. (See Chapter 7 for specific ideas about making evangelism a priority in the life of your group.)

> *You are here for a purpose; otherwise God would have already brought you home to Him.*

God sent Jesus into the world as the Good Shepherd who compassionately seeks after His lost sheep. He has called you as his undershepherd to prayerfully rely on God's provision and to turn your compassion into action. Now He is sending you to seek and to save the lost just as the Father sent Him (John 17:18).

Heart to Heart

1. Read Matthew 9:9-10:5. Describe Jesus' heart from this passage.

2. The attribute's of Jesus' heart were listed in the chapter: an authentic heart, a servant's heart, a compassionate heart, a shepherd's heart, a heart connected to God, and a disciple-making heart. Talk briefly about each one. How can you grow in each area?

3. Look again at the "Shepherd/Hired Hand" table. Do you consider yourself a shepherd or a hired hand? Why?

4. How can you grow in becoming a more Christ-like leader? What steps will you take?

Chapter Three

A Heart Empowered and Led by the Holy Spirit

When Samuel anointed David, the Bible says that "from that day on the Spirit of the Lord came upon David in power" (1 Samuel 16:13). David walked with and was led by the Spirit throughout his leadership of Israel, beginning even when he battled Goliath. David told the giant soldier, "You come against me with sword and spear and javelin, but I come against you in the name of the Lord Almighty . . . for the battle is the Lord's and he will give all of you into our hands" (1 Samuel 17:45-47).

First Chronicles 11 records David becoming king of Israel and the exploits of him and his mighty men. Before conquering Jerusalem, the Jebusite people who lived there told him, "You will not get in here" (1 Chronicles 11:5). In other words, "You ain't got what it takes to beat us. We're big and strong and our city is fortified. Na na na na na na!" In the parallel passage of 2 Samuel 5:6, the people are recorded as adding, "Even the blind and the lame can ward you off." Apparently, they did not know much about David and the strength that came from His God.

"Nevertheless," both passages say, "David captured the fortress of Zion, the City of David." Not only did he and his men do what was said could not be done, he got the chance to rub it in a little when the city was named after him!

The Jebusites talked a good game, but there was no power behind their words. They did not have the kind of power that was behind David and his army. The whole scene could be summarized by Paul's words in 1 Corinthians 4:20: "For the kingdom of God is not a matter of talk but of power." Or as stated in 1 Chronicles 11:9, "David became more and more powerful, because the Lord Almighty was with him."

David's mighty men followed his leadership. They were mighty because the Lord Almighty was with them. Jashobeam killed 300 men with his spear in one encounter. Three hundred against one. Sounds like a *Rambo* movie or *Mission Impossible.* And it was, humanly speaking. But wait, "What is impossible with men is possible with God" (Luke 18:27). "Everything is possible for him who believes" (Mark 9:23). "I can do everything through him who gives me strength" (Philippians 4:13).

Eleazar was another of David's mighty men. He was "with David when they taunted the Philistines gathered at Pas Dammim for battle" (2 Samuel 23:9). The battle was so fierce that the rest of the Israelite army retreated, leaving David and Eleazar alone in a barley field. "But they took their stand in the middle of the field. They defended it and struck the Philistines down, and the Lord brought about a great victory" (1 Chronicles 11:14).

> *As people who have the Holy Spirit living within us, we have every reason to have courage in everything we do.*

Eleazar fought so hard and long that his muscles locked his hand to his weapon: "He held his ground and struck down the Philistines till his hand grew tired and froze to the sword" (2 Samuel 23:10). What a warrior! Even John Wayne would be proud. But wait. Again we are reminded, "The Lord brought about a great victory that day."

We need reminders: "Do not be afraid or discouraged because of this vast army. For the battle is not yours, but God's" (2 Chronicles 20:15). "Be strong and courageous. Do not be afraid or discouraged because of the king of Assyria and the vast army with him, for there is a greater power with us than with him. With him is only the arm of flesh, but with us is the Lord our God to help us and to fight our battles" (2 Chronicles 32:7-8). "'Not by [human] might nor by [human] power, but by my Spirit,' says the Lord Almighty" (Zechariah 4:6). "The one who is in you is greater than the one who is in the world" (1 John 4:4). As people who have the Holy Spirit living within us providing all we need, we have every reason to have courage in everything we do.

Keep the Spiritual Fervor!

"Let's do something so big that if God isn't in it, it is destined to fail!" I write this saying on the white board in my office every once in a while to remind everyone— especially myself — to be a holy risk taker.

Before I became a Christian, I worked as an inventory control auditor for a retail store chain. I was like many of my friends, going to our jobs every day, coming home to eat dinner, watching a little TV, and going to bed, just to get up the next morning to do it all over again. What a boring existence!

After becoming a Christian, I found that even church services can be boring if all we do is congregate every Sunday morning. I've been a part of a small group or two that were not much more interesting. Same day, same time. Same place, same people. Only the Bible passage changes.

Where's the passion you had when you were a new Christian? What happened to the sense of purpose God gave you when He called you to Himself? Where is the vision that your Father put inside you for His kingdom? Maybe you need a dose of Romans 12:11: "Never be lacking in zeal, but keep your spiritual fervor, serving the Lord."

The apostle Peter is a good example of someone who lived life with passion. At times his passion was misguided, nonetheless, he lived life to the fullest. The first time we see Peter in the book of Luke is in chapter 5; he meets Jesus in a boat, and Jesus changes Peter's entire outlook on life.

In verse 5, Peter was faced with a conflict. Here was a religious leader who used to be a carpenter telling Peter the *fisherman* how to fish! Peter could have said, "Look, Jesus, you stick with teaching and woodworking and let me do the fishing here. I've been doing it for years. I know what I'm doing!" But Peter did what Jesus said simply because Jesus said

> *Anyone can live with zeal and passion. But if that zeal is directed by God, it is much more satisfying and productive.*

to do it. That must have taken tremendous faith for Peter. He had probably heard Jesus preach, but he did not know very much about Jesus yet. Peter was available to be used by Jesus; he was faithful in doing what Jesus asked, even if it sounded preposterous.

Peter's fishing had been fruitless (actually, fishless) without Jesus. But with Jesus in his boat, Peter flourished beyond expectation. It's the same for us today. With His Holy Spirit guiding us, we will be abundantly fruitful.

Anyone can live with zeal and passion. But if that zeal is directed by God, it is much more satisfying and productive. People have passions for many things in life: sports, cars, hobbies, favorite television shows, jobs, and many more.

Peter had a passion for fishing. But he had never experienced such a thrill fishing as he did when Jesus stepped into his boat that day. Jesus can do the same thing for us and our passions. He can turn an ordinary job into an adventure. He can turn an ordinary small group into an extraordinary community.

What do you have a passion for? Sports have always been one of my passions. I love playing all kinds of sports: softball, basketball, and golf, and I am extremely competitive. When I first became a Christian, I had to ask myself how I could allow Jesus to have lordship over sports in my life. The verse, "Whatever you do, work at it with all your heart, as working for the Lord, not for men" (Colossians 3:23), gave me perspective. So I decided to play every game as for God.

My Christian friends and I started playing basketball with a purpose. We'd go to the local playgrounds and get involved in games with the goal of developing relationships with other players. Each of us would pray for the guy we were guarding, and look for God-given opportunities to reach out. As we developed friendships, we invited the guys to open-gym basketball at our church building. Jesus enabled us to be "fishers of men" on the basketball courts! He took lordship over our passion for basketball and used it to redeem people far from Him.

In verse 8, after Peter saw the great catch of fish and Jesus' power displayed, Peter fell down at Jesus' feet and said, in effect, "I'm not worthy. I'm a sinful man. Lord, I'm not worthy to even have you in my boat." Peter recognized his own sinfulness and realized that he was in the presence of someone great and powerful.

I can see Peter doing this, can't you? With all of his zeal and passion, Peter held nothing back. Notice, he didn't try to explain the miracle away or take credit for the catch of fish. He knew from where the power came.

I may have a passion for doing something for the Lord, but I constantly need to be reminded that it is *God* who does the work through *His* power. I have had the opportunity to be a part of helping people turn their lives over to the Lord. It is one of the most rewarding things in life. But it is not I who brings about the changes in people's hearts. It is God's Spirit that changes them from the inside out. I am merely God's representative — doing what He has called me to do.

In verse 11 Peter is transformed from a fisher of *fish* into a fisher of *men*. Being a fisher of fish is a valuable job, just as being an accountant, waitress, electrician, or secretary is valuable. Yet they all pale in comparison to the "business" of fishing for people, because people matter to God.

Peter *acted* upon his beliefs. He didn't just sit back and say, "Yeah, Jesus, I think it's great what you're trying to do here. But I'm pretty comfortable here in my fishing business. I'm sure others can help you with this "fishing for men" thing. Take my brother, Andrew, here."

In Cincinnati, where I was born and raised, we had a little newspaper called *The Downtowner*. Every month they interviewed people who worked downtown for a feature called Miss or Mr. Downtowner.

One of the questions asked of a particular Miss Downtowner was, "What is the one thing you'd most like to see?"

Miss Downtowner answered, "More homeless shelters."

Later in the interview they asked, "What would you do if you won the lottery?"

She responded, "I'd buy an island and throw a huge party for all my friends."

Miss Downtowner had a cause, but she wasn't willing to pay the cost herself. Her actions didn't match her so-called passion for the poor.

Peter wasn't a hypocrite, however. He left everything he had ever known to enter the unknown. As small group leaders, we must step out of our comfort zones to follow the challenge Jesus gives us as we follow Him.

I can relate to Peter. I became a Christian at the age of 28. I was doing very well in my job, climbing the corporate ladder. When I became a Christian, all my values changed. I felt a tug on my heart to do something bigger with my life. So I started praying that God would allow me to serve Him in the way He wanted me to.

Soon after that, I lost my job when the company I worked for went through a hostile takeover. I was asked to interview with another retail chain in Chicago, making twice as much as I made at my previous job. I turned it down. I saw losing my job as an opportunity to do something special with my life for God. So, four months after becoming a Christian, I became a full-time student at Cincinnati Bible Seminary. Like Peter, I stepped out of my boat to become a fisher of men.

Most of us don't need to leave our jobs in order to serve God. In fact, some of the most strategic places to serve Him are where we are right now. As Tony Evans says, "If you are an accountant, you're not just an accountant; you're God's representative in the accounting field. If you're a secretary, you're not just a secretary, you're God's representative in the office. If you're a student, you're not just a student; you're God's representative in the school."

> *As small group leaders, we must be willing to step out of our comfort zones to follow the challenge Jesus gives us as we follow Him.*

Please don't miss one important fact. Peter didn't become a fisher of people by himself. Matthew and Mark's Gospel accounts both record Jesus telling Peter, "*I* will make you fishers of men."

Peter was outgoing, but he was rough around the edges. He spoke before thinking things through. His foot often ended up in his mouth. He wasn't the most eloquent spokesman for God. But he had raw material for Jesus to work with. He was willing and faithful. He could be humbled. He was willing to change. He had a heart for God and a heart for people.

After Jesus' death, burial, and resurrection, the disciples were sitting around a room together; Peter got up and said, "Hey guys, I'm going fishing" (see John 21). Perhaps he just wanted to get his mind off of things. Maybe the money they had depended on before the crucifixion was not available anymore. It's interesting that Peter chose to go back to what he did before Jesus called him. It's almost as if Peter was saying, "I've really failed. I denied that I even knew Jesus, and He was my friend, my Lord. Besides that, he *tried* telling us he'd die and rise again, but I missed the whole thing. I'm a failure. I'm going back to what I know: fishing for fish. *That* I can do."

So he went out on the boat with his buddies and they fished . . . and fished . . . and fished . . . and caught nothing.

> There are times in our lives Jesus that we too fail Jesus; He is always there to restore us and return us to what He has called us to.

Suddenly they heard a voice from the shore. "Hey, friends, don't you have any fish?"

"Nope!"

"Throw your net on the right side of the boat, and you'll find some."

The disciples looked at each other. Then they tugged in the empty net and threw it on the other side of the boat. The net filled with so many fish that they couldn't even pull it back in. "Hasn't this happened before, guys?"

Before the rest of them knew it, Peter was jumping into the water and swimming ashore.

When he got there, Jesus was waiting for him. He was there to restore him and to forgive him. But also, I think, to get him refocused. Three times Jesus told Peter, basically, to take care of people. "People matter to God," Jesus was saying to him, "and I want them to matter to you too. I have called you to follow Me as a shepherd, and I want your passion to be fishing for people, not fishing for fish, Peter. I want you to throw your life into being a fisher of men."

There are times in our lives that we too fail Jesus; He is always there to restore us and return us to what He has called us to. In my ministry, I have needed Jesus' restoration and refocusing more than I would like to admit. I get off track, thinking that something else can give me what I need. He says to me, "Hey friend, don't you have what you're fishing for?" Nope. He says, "Try doing it my way again." He has taught me this lesson over and over again in my life. When will I really learn?

If you are like me, and I suspect that you are, then perhaps you too need Jesus to bring you back to His plan for your life now and again. He reminds us what He has called us to do: "Take care of my sheep."

Before His death, Jesus promised that after He went away the Father would send the Holy Spirit. The role of the Spirit would be to teach them all things (John 14:26), convict the world of guilt in regard to sin and righteousness and judgment (16:8), and guide believers into all truth (16:13). The disciples received power to be His witnesses when the Holy Spirit came upon them (Acts 1:8).

The Spirit enabled the disciples to take holy risks. On the day of Pentecost, just 50 days after Jesus' crucifixion, Peter stood up and told his Jewish listeners that they, with the help of wicked men, had put Jesus to death. Soon after that, in another sermon on the streets of Jerusalem, he went so far as to tell the Jews that they and their leaders had acted in ignorance.

> *The Holy Spirit still gives ordinary Christians like you and me the power to take holy risks and to step out in faith with courage and determination.*

When brought before the Jewish council, the disciples' holy boldness only intensified. The rulers, elders, and teachers of the law asked them, "By what power or what name did you do this?" "Then Peter, filled with the Holy Spirit, said to them, '. . . It is by the name of Jesus Christ of Nazareth, whom you crucified but whom God raised from the dead, that this man stands before you healed'" (Acts 4:7-10).

The narrative continues, "When they saw the courage of Peter and John and realized they were unschooled, ordinary men, they were astonished and took note that these men had been with Jesus" (Acts 4:7-13). God uses ordinary people to do extraordinary things. By using unschooled, ordinary people He reveals *His* power and glory.

The Holy Spirit still gives ordinary Christians like you and me the power to take holy risks and to step out in faith with courage and determination.

We're Not Mere Men

So where is that faith and courage and zeal in today's church? Where is the growth and intensity the early house churches experienced? Is the Holy Spirit inactive? Has Jesus broken His promise that He would build His church and that He would never leave us nor forsake us?

No. The problem is not with God, but with us. We've settled for lukewarm faith. We don't act like people empowered by God's Spirit. We act like "mere men."

When Paul wrote to the floundering church in Corinth, he asked them, "Are you not acting like mere men?" As Christians, we *are* more than mere men. We have the Holy Spirit living within us. We are God's children, His representatives. He has bought us with a price and we belong to Him. *Nothing* is impossible for us if we believe.

> *As small group leaders we are in a spiritual battle for people's hearts and souls.*

Small group leaders are called to live as more than mere men, with passion for Christ, zeal for His word, and spiritual fervor for His commission. They are holy risk takers who model that lifestyle for those in the group. They step out in faith and are ready to throw their lives into serving God wherever and however God calls them. They have surrendered their lives to Him.

Small group leaders are in a spiritual battle for people's hearts and souls. "For our struggle is not against flesh and blood, but against the rulers, against the authorities, against the powers of this dark world and against the spiritual forces of evil in the heavenly realms" (Ephesians 6:12). Because we are God's representatives, we have the right and the power to confront these forces in His name. We are not mere men!

There is more to existence than our limited minds can comprehend; we must realize that the spiritual realm is true and has power. The Holy Spirit is as real as the book you are reading. As a child of God, the Spirit has taken up residence in your life and provides extraordinary power to and through you. You are no mere man or woman. You are called not only to a Spirit-filled life, but also to a Spirit-led, Spirit-anointed, Spirit-powered life.

More Than Mere Bible Studies

I wonder if many of our churches and small groups have become like the churches of Sardis and Laodicea. They have the reputation of being alive, but they are dead. Their deeds are not complete in the sight of God because they are not fulfilling His mission. They are neither cold nor hot, but lukewarm. They believe they are rich because they study the Bible and pray together, but they do not realize they are wretched, pitiful, poor, blind, and naked. The power of the Holy Spirit is missing from these churches and groups.

Jesus stands outside the door of the homes where small groups meet and knocks. "Let me in!" He cries. He has empowered us with His Spirit to be His witnesses to the ends of the earth, yet some of us sit in our cozy homes, not willing to carry the Good News down the street, much less around the world.

We are so busy "doing Bible study" that we do not have the time or interest to do what the Bible says.

Would Jesus spit us out of His mouth if He were to observe what happens (or doesn't happen) in most of our groups? Is He waiting to return because His church has not fulfilled His commission?

It's time to wake up our small groups and allow the Holy Spirit to transform them into true spiritual families that minister by the Spirit's power. That means getting out of our safe routines and letting God take control. Like young David facing Goliath, God meets us on the field of battle and provides us with everything we need to be victorious in His name. When we surrender our lives to Him, He empowers us and uses us to fight His fights. His power is available to us though we are powerless by ourselves, but we must step out of our comfort zones and let His power work!

> When we surrender our lives to Him, He empowers us and uses us to fight His fights.

A Christian small group is more than a meeting, more than a Bible discussion, and more than a social event. Before we can come to a true understanding of what a small group is, it is helpful to discuss what one is not:

- *A club.* Some groups are arranged around an affinity: young moms, retirees, newly married couples, etc. But every small group has a purpose beyond its affinity. A Christian group exists to glorify God and make disciples. Different groups find varied ways of doing that.
- *A clique or closed membership "secret society."* We get close to one another — beyond the surface level stuff — but we always look outward to include others in our community. The mission of a small group is to make disciples.
- *An organization.* An organization consists of individuals who are intentionally and sometimes artificially organized into some sort of groupings. A small group is a *living organism.* It is a natural and distinctive part of the body of Christ.
- *Static.* If a group does not multiply itself, it dies. In the same way, a small group must continually reproduce itself. Small groups are designed to reach out to unbelievers, raise up new leadership from within, and multiply by birthing new groups.
- *One day a week.* A small group is more than just another once-a-week meeting. The members of the group *share life together* as a family. The meeting is family-reunion time. The rest of the week, group members naturally pastor one another — visiting, making phone calls, having dinner together, serving together, shopping together, and more.
- *A class.* Small groups practice Colossians 3:16: "Let the word of Christ dwell

in you richly as you teach and admonish one another with all wisdom." The group leader is more shepherd than teacher. He is not the group's answer man, but one who *facilitates* the teaching and admonishing of one another.

• *Just a "Bible study."* We study God's Word with an eye toward putting it into action. "Do not merely listen to the word, and so deceive yourselves. Do what it says" (James 1:22). Small groups put the Bible into action!

• *A therapy group.* Members of small groups care for one another, but this caring is not meant to turn into psychoanalysis sessions. When a member has a need, the group responds with care and prayer . . . *period!* They do not offer advice unless it is asked for.

• *A band of renegades.* Each group is connected with other groups and with the overall mission and ministry of the church. Leaders receive centralized support and training. Groups work together to carry out the church's mission. They are accountable to leadership to keep things on track. The group is an integral part of the whole body of Christ.

The real leader of a small group is the Holy Spirit. The person we often call the leader is only a human facilitator of the Spirit's leadership. That has huge implications for the shepherd-leader's role and what happens in the group's meeting times.

A "leader," as defined secularly, must maintain control of discussion and all of the group's plans. A facilitator, or shepherd-leader, on the other hand, gently guides the group, while the Spirit leads the facilitator. This distinction may mean that the facilitator changes the agenda if it is not in line with what God has planned for the meeting time. This can be a huge leap for some small group leaders. Some of us feel like we must be in control at all times.

We've acquired a debilitating disease called agenda-itus. Its symptoms for those afflicted are numerous: drowsiness, inattention, spiritual starvation, legalism. It happens when a facilitator sticks so tightly to his or her agenda that the group suffers.

Having an agenda can be helpful. An agenda keeps us on track. It provides purpose and direction. Most people don't want to show up for a meeting and have the leader say, "So, what do you all want to talk about tonight?" I've been in meetings like that. Meetings in which the facilitator failed to facilitate. Meetings that went nowhere because the leader had no plan and no direction.

The other extreme is just as bad, if not worse. God has made it very clear in His Word that our plans amount to nothing when separated from His purpose. When we make our plans according to His will and purpose they can make an eternal difference.[1]

There's nothing wrong with us as leaders making plans, but we must be sensitive to the moving of the Holy Spirit as we facilitate. If we carry out our own plans — plans that are not God's plans — He says we are "obstinate children" (Isaiah 30:1)!

Sometimes, I have an agenda set for a meeting, but the Holy Spirit has something else in mind for that night. So I set aside my agenda, while the Spirit leads, and prayerfully try to keep in step with Him. This seems dangerous to some of us. As Jim Cymbala has said, "God the Holy Spirit does unusual things, and he does not always notify us in advance."[2]

> *The real leader of a small group is the Holy Spirit.*

A young woman shows up and begins crying during the icebreaker. A couple reveals that they are having problems in their marriage. Someone shares a prayer request for a parent who is dying, or a spouse or child who is very sick. A man in the group has lost his job. A variety of situations can crop up that mean throwing out the agenda — or at least part of it — for the meeting. Or perhaps as you pray before the meeting, the Spirit puts something on your heart that is not on your agenda. Or in the facilitating of the study, a tangent arises that you sense is more important than the study itself, and the Spirit urges you to discuss the subject more.

What do you do? You follow the Spirit's leading!

How do you know the Spirit's leading? You spend a lot of time with the Spirit — studying the Word, praying in quiet meditation, getting away from the rush to listen to God speak to you. You stay connected to the Vine (John 15).

More Than Mere Teaching, Less Than Real Teachers

In John 15 and 16, Jesus called the Holy Spirit the "Counselor." What does a counselor do? He counsels! If the Holy Spirit is the real teacher, we are merely the vessels through which He operates. But not if we stick to our agendas, with no regard for His leading.

One word of warning. While you need to be sensitive to the Spirit's leading in regard to moving from your agenda, be sensitive to the moving of other spiritual forces as well. A facilitator can get into trouble by straying from the agenda too much. He or she may allow trivialities to take over the meeting. Some members will grow weary, sensing that the group is moving in no direction. Be aware of Satan's craftiness. He wants to influence you and distract you with little things, get you off an important subject, and keep you focused on the wrong things.

In the early church, some teachers, particularly the Gnostics, who taught that knowledge is supreme, were advancing false doctrine. Salvation, they asserted, was gained not by faith in Christ but by special knowledge. The apostle John wrote his first letter especially to warn Christians about this. Our most reliable teacher, John said, is the Holy Spirit:

> *I am writing these things to you about those who are trying to lead you astray. As for you, the anointing you received from him remains in you, and you do not need anyone else to teach you. But as his anointing teaches you about all things and as that anointing is real, not counterfeit — just as it has taught you, remain in him. (1 John 2:26-27)*

Part of the Holy Spirit's ministry to and through us is this teaching ministry. Jesus said, "the Counselor, the Holy Spirit, whom the Father will send in my name, will teach you all things" (John 14:26). When we follow His lead, He will guide us into all truth (John 16:13; here, as in other passages, the Holy Spirit is called the "Spirit of truth").

The Christian recipients of Jude's letter were also warned about false teachers who could lead them astray. Jude said that those men "follow mere natural instincts and do not have the Spirit" (Jude 19). Intelligence, wisdom, knowledge, skills, and even natural instincts are not what it takes to be a godly leader. Godly leadership takes a heart that is attentive and willing to follow the Spirit.

> *Satan wants to influence you and distract you with little things, get you off an important subject, and keep you focused on the wrong things.*

In *Experiencing God,* Blackaby and King put it eloquently:

> Now that the Holy Spirit is given, He is the One who guides you into all truth and teaches you all things. You understand spiritual truth because the Holy Spirit is working in your life. You cannot understand the Word of God unless the Spirit of God teaches you. When you come to the Word of God, the Author Himself is present to instruct you. You never discover truth; truth is revealed. When the Holy Spirit reveals truth to you, He is not leading you to an encounter with God. That is an encounter with God![3]

In the first two chapters of 1 Corinthians, Paul argued that knowledge and wisdom are not as essential as the power of the Holy Spirit. He begins by saying the "message of the cross is foolishness to those who are perishing [without Christ], but to us who are being saved it is the power of God" (1 Corinthians 1:18). He goes on to ask, "Where is the wise man? Where is the scholar? Where is the philosopher of this age? Has not God made foolish the wisdom of the world?" (1 Corinthians 1:20). Later Paul says, "My message and my preaching were not with wise and persuasive words, but with a demonstration of the Spirit's power, so that your faith may not rest on men's wisdom, but on God's power" (1 Corinthians 2:4).

This passage has at least three important implications for small group leaders: power, not words, will make the biggest impact; a godly heart, not just skills, will make the strongest leader; and God uses ordinary people to accomplish the extraordinary for Him.

Power, Not Words

Wise and persuasive words will not win our neighborhoods and workplaces and society to Christ. A witness with wise words but no spiritual power is a weak witness. People may come to the Lord through knowledge-based teaching, but when they do, their faith is more dependent on the teacher's "wisdom" than God's power.

I've seen this. A person comes to Christ through the insightful teaching of a preacher, teacher, or evangelist. They become part of the church and show up at meetings Sunday morning and evening and Wednesday evening, or whenever the preacher who brought them to Christ is speaking. They "go to church" for years without ever really growing up. As the writer of Hebrews puts it, by this time they ought to be teachers, but they need someone to teach them the elementary truths of God's word all over again. They need milk, not solid food! The image I get is a preacher pushing back the whiskers of a mature believer to shove in a baby bottle. These are the people who say, "I just want to be fed!" The problem is that they should be able to feed themselves! In fact, they should be feeding others.

A small group leader who depends on words, knowledge, and wisdom falls into the same trap. This is not to say our words are not important or that we should not share the Good News with those around us. God's Word clearly tells us to do so. Instead those words must emanate from God's wisdom and power, not our own.

We have not received the spirit of the world but the Spirit who is from God, that we may understand what God has freely given us. This is what we speak, not in words taught us by human wisdom but in words taught by the Spirit, expressing spiritual truths in spiritual words.

(1 Corinthians 2:12-13)

Heart, Not Skills

Often, when small group ministers look for leaders or when leaders look for interns, they look at outside things like how much of the Bible a person knows, how intelligent or humanly wise they are, or if they are a good teacher. It is more important to look at the person's heart. Are they people after God's heart? Do they demonstrate the Spirit's power in their lives? Do they walk with the Spirit and follow the Spirit's lead?

People often decline a request to facilitate a small group because of a faulty understanding of what a small group leader is and does:

FAULTY VIEW: The small group leader . . .	BIBLICAL VIEW
Is seminary trained or has lots of knowledge of the Scriptures, theology, apologetics, and counseling.	The apostles Peter and John astonished the onlookers because they were "unschooled, ordinary" men with great courage and power from the Holy Spirit.
Has special spiritual gifts, particularly leadership, administration, and teaching.	Some of the best facilitators lead using gifts of mercy, shepherding, encouragement, helps, creative communication, and others.
Is an extrovert and natural teacher.	Is more of a shepherd and facilitator.

God Uses Ordinary People to Accomplish Extraordinary Things

Spiritual leadership is more about the Spirit's power than skills, talents, abilities, and other "outward appearances." God uses ordinary people to do extraordinary things by His power.

Let's face it: ordinary Christians abound! This is good news, because God uses them to grow His church. But the church must open up spiritual leadership to these unschooled, ordinary people and allow them to develop other ordinary people to multiply the ministry and grow God's church. The priesthood of all believers is critical to unleashing the Spirit's power in extraordinary ways to build the kingdom of God.

While leadership remains in the hands of the few, the growth of the kingdom will be stunted and many people will die without coming to know Christ as Savior. It's time to mobilize, and "disciplize"! That's our calling, church. That's our commission. Let's go!

Heart to Heart

1. What do you think is the relationship between being empowered and led by the Holy Spirit and the ability of a person to lead with courage and passion?

2. In practical terms, what does it mean to you to be more than a mere man or woman?

3. If the "real" leader of the cell is the Holy Spirit, what is your role? How can you grow in your reliance on the Holy Spirit so that you can follow His leading as you make plans and facilitate cell meetings?

Chapter Four

The Heart of the Call

David was just minding his own business. He was a shepherd. Nothing glamorous. Nothing special. He expected nothing more than his lot in life. However, God had other plans. He had a purpose for David's life.

God called David to leadership. David did not deserve it or earn it. It was a gift of God's grace according to His sovereign purpose. David did not climb some leadership ladder or work his way up the pecking order. God chose him and called him to His service, because David was a man after God's own heart.

When given the opportunity to take over the reigns of leadership, he passed. He understood that it was not right to take the life of the standing king, even though David had been anointed as the next king. He was willing to wait on God. The call was His.

When I first felt called to ministry and started interviewing for a church leadership position in 1995, my wife confided in me that she was not ready yet to be a "pastor's wife." That helped me realize I was not ready to be a pastor either. God was not going to call me without my wife, and I recognized that the "call" I was feeling was not from God.

I stopped interviewing with churches and remained in the place that God had called me to at that time as a writer and dot-com entrepreneur. Two years later, I sensed God moving us in a new direction. I felt a leading to be involved in the "front lines" of ministry, working in the local church. While attending the North American Christian Convention, senior pastors from three churches approached me about coming on staff with them.

When I got home, my wife and I discussed the possibility of going into full-time staff ministry. The phone rang in the middle of our conversation, and Heidi answered. It was one of the pastors that I had talked to at the convention. I took the phone from her hand and asked, "Are you OK with this?" She said yes. "Are you sure you're ready?" She said, "Go for it!" Heidi felt the same leading I felt. God was moving us out of the safe and comfortable and into a new purpose for Him. A few months later, we were loading our earthly belongings into trucks and cars to move to central Indiana. When God calls you into His service, you pack up and move!

> *A person becomes a leader in the church by the gift of God's grace.*

A person becomes a leader in the church by the gift of God's grace. It is not something we attain or deserve. It is given to us for the working of His power according to His eternal purpose.

God calls all kinds of people to his service. Perhaps we think only staff pastors receive a calling or anointing, but Scripture does not reflect this thought. The Bible clearly shows that all Christians receive a calling from God.

Calling as a Gift

The apostle Paul showed a godly heart when he said, "I became a servant of this gospel by the gift of God's grace given me through the working of his power" (Ephesians 3:7). As servants of the gospel, we must realize that our calling is a *gift* given us to give to others. Too many times, leadership is grabbed rather than accepted as a gift of God's grace. If I had taken a church staff position the first time I was asked to interview, I would have been doing so on my own, not as a result of God's purpose for my life. God has a plan for your life, Christian. Be sure that you, like Paul, become a servant of the gospel by the gift of God's grace through the working of His power.

Paul explains that God's intention in calling him as a servant of the gospel "was that now, through the church, the manifold wisdom of God should be made known . . . according to his eternal purpose" (Ephesians 3:10-11). There is always a sovereign purpose behind God's call on an individual's life. You may not immediately know that purpose, but that does not really matter. What matters is how you respond to His call.

Beginning in verse 14 of chapter 3, Paul prays an eloquent prayer for the Ephesian Christians revealing the calling God had put on their lives. Read through this passage and notice the progression of the prayer.

1. *"out of his glorious riches"* — All worthwhile ministry begins with what God has already provided and with what He is already doing.

2. *"He may strengthen you with power through His Spirit"* — All of the power for our ministry comes from God through the working of the Holy Spirit in our lives.

3. *"in your inner being"* — Not only does God call people after His own heart, He builds on that godly heart by strengthening it with His power.

4. *"so that Christ may dwell in your hearts through faith"* — Since this prayer was for the *believers* in Ephesus, we know that Christ was already indwelling their hearts through faith. So why did Paul pray these words? He was asking that Christ be completely at home in every part of their lives. A called person never stops growing in faith.

5. *"I pray that you, being rooted and established in love, may have power"* — Paul uses the words "love" and "power" three times each in this brief passage. These two attributes are the keys to a called person's ministry.

6. *"love that surpasses knowledge"* — The greatest of all the gifts God gives is love. "Knowledge puffs up, but love builds up" (1 Corinthians 8:1). Intellectualism is not a prerequisite for being called by God to ministry. Love is.

7. *"that you may be filled to the measure of all the fullness of God"* — This is where the power and love comes from. God's means are limitless. He makes His resources available to all of those He calls.

8. *"to him who is able to do immeasurably more than all we ask or imagine, according to his power that is at work within us"* — God's power in those He calls is more than we can imagine. We have no excuse for failure when that power is at work within us.

9. *"to him be glory in the church and in Christ Jesus"* — Our calling, our service, our ministry, and our existence, are for His glory, not our own.

10. *"throughout all generations, forever and ever! Amen."* — While our service is limited to our lifetime, the effects of that ministry, and the glory God receives from it are eternal. God's call on our lives is part of His infinite purpose for His world and His kingdom.

Paul begins chapter 4 of his letter to the Ephesians by urging them "to live a life worthy of the calling you have received." This admonition was for all of the believers in Ephesus, not just the preachers and elders of the church. Then Paul tells them how to live out their calling: "Be completely humble and gentle; be patient, bearing with one another in love. Make every effort to keep the unity of the Spirit through the bond of peace" (4:1-3). These are all the internal, heart qualities a called person possesses.

The Called Person

In his classic book, *Ordering Your Private World* — a must-read for every small group leader or intern — Gordon MacDonald devotes a chapter to "Living as a Called Person." His insightful thoughts form a foundation for what I want to share in this section.

MacDonald points out that "called men and women can come from the strangest places and carry the most unique qualifications. They may be the unnoticed, the unappreciated, the unsophisticated."[1] They can be the unschooled, ordinary people who have spent time with Jesus. (Of course, that does not *exclude* educated people from ministry!) The men that Jesus called to be His disciples are good examples of this point. I can personally attest to the fact that Jesus still calls people from the strangest places with the most unique qualifications today!

MacDonald uses John the Baptist as a striking picture of a called person. From the very beginning of his ministry, John knew who he was and what God had called him to. He lived his life with a vivid sense of mission, purpose, and destiny.

The Called Person Lives Within His or Her Own Calling

John did not try to be more than he was. "I am not the Christ, but am sent ahead of him," he said (John 3:28). With all the popularity he was gaining and power he was displaying, John easily could have said, "Well, now that you mention it, maybe I *am* the Christ." That was not John's heart. Even though the crowds were praising him and wondering if he could be the Christ, the Prophet, or Elijah, he had no Messiah Complex! He lived within his own calling from God. He knew he was "the voice of one calling in the desert, 'Make straight the way of the Lord'" (John 1:23) but Jesus was the "Lamb of God who takes away the sin of the world" (John 1:29).

The Called Person Is Committed to His or Her Calling

When people were leaving John to follow Jesus, John responded, "That joy is mine, and it is now complete." When someone recruits you to a job that you are not called to, it's easy to throw in the towel when the going gets tough. When you are sure of your calling from God and you know you represent Him, your commitment allows you to continue regardless of the circumstances.

When God called Heidi and I to move across the country from Indiana to Idaho, several of our relatives and friends could not comprehend how we could move our kids away from their grandparents, aunts, uncles, and cousins. We explained that our commitment to God prompted and guided our actions. We knew He was calling us to Idaho at this point in our lives. Like Abraham, we "obeyed and went," even though we did not know where we were going. We knew we would be like strangers in a foreign country, at first anyway (Hebrews 11:8-9). Like the Apostle Paul, we went not knowing what would happen to us here (Acts 20:22). Our commitment to God ruled over any possible circumstances or consequences.

The Called Person Is a Steward

John the Baptist had a proper understanding of stewardship. When the crowds began leaving John to follow Jesus, John could have become angry and controlling. Instead he said, "A man can receive only what has been given to him from heaven" (John 4:27). The people who asked John about the crowd's transfer of affections assumed that the crowds *belonged* to John, that he was losing

> *When you are sure of your calling from God and you know you represent Him, your commitment allows you to continue regardless of the circumstances.*

something — like power and prestige — as the crowds left him. But that was not John's perspective at all. John knew that he did not own *anything*, much less the crowds!

John's heart was the heart of a steward. A steward manages the owner's assets or accounts until the owner returns. John knew that the crowds who were leaving him for Jesus were never his in the first place. His calling was to be a wise and faithful servant with what God put him in charge of until Jesus came along. He played his part and then graciously stepped out of the way.

You may not have been given stewardship over crowds as John was, but perhaps God has given you charge over other things:
- "Your" career.
- "Your" finances.
- "Your" health.
- "Your" spiritual gifts.
- "Your" small group.
- "Your" _____.

Think about this for a moment. How would your attitude and actions change if you were to think of these things the same way John thought of the crowds — with stewardship eyes?

As you prepare for your next small group meeting, spend time in prayer with the Master and Owner of the group. Prayerfully acknowledge that the group is His, the people are His, the time is His. Ask for His power as you prepare to facilitate the group. He has entrusted you with the stewardship of the group, so receive the group as God's gift and charge to you from heaven. Be like the wise servants given talents by their master in Jesus' parable in Matthew 25:14-30, and gain more than He has entrusted you with. Grow your small group by making disciples.

The unwise servant in the parable, who only returned to the master what belonged to him in the first place, is akin to the small group leader who never takes any risks with his group. He never sends them out to reach out to others. He fails to invest what God has entrusted him with for the sake of the kingdom.

God has chosen to allow you to manage His investments of people, time, and resources. What kind of return are you providing on His investment?

The Called Person Is a Humble Servant

John remained humble — he had a servant's heart. In Matthew 11:11, Jesus said "among those born of women [everyone!], there has not risen anyone greater than John the Baptist." That included Abraham, Moses, David, and the prophets. John was given an incredible job: to pave the way for the awaited Messiah. He had multitudes following him and obeying him. He was "da man"!

> *He has entrusted you with the stewardship of the group, so receive the group as God's gift and charge to you from heaven.*

John knew and respected his unique position in the kingdom of God. "[Jesus] must become greater; I must become less," (John 3:30). He was a called man, not a driven man. A driven person always wants more power, wealth, attention, and status. I know. Before God redeemed my life, I was a driven man. I worked hard to attain a certain level of success in my career, but it all was empty without God. Even after becoming a Christian, I still have to watch out for "drivenness" in my life. It can be an addiction and it is a temptation to move away from a dependence on God.

In the busyness and noise of the clamoring crowds, in all the attention and prestige and position, it is all too easy to miss the still, small voice of God calling us. Called people are content with what God provides and use all of it for His glory. When the adulation of the crowd becomes deafening, the voice of God becomes even louder for called people.

For John, the clamoring of the crowds, the public attention, and the praises of his followers never drowned out the voice of God. John's inner world — his private world — was in order. So when the external world pushed in on him, he stayed true to his calling. Perhaps that is why Jesus called him the greatest person who ever lived. But don't miss the next thing Jesus said: "yet he who is least in the kingdom of heaven is greater than he" (Matthew 11:11). John was great because he was willing to become less. We can be even "greater" if we are willing to be the "least."

> *God accomplishes extraordinary things through the humble, committed stewards He calls into His service.*

Small group leadership is a high calling. God accomplishes extraordinary things through the humble, committed stewards He calls into His service.

How to Live a Called Life

Who is in control of your destiny? From where or whom do you get your sense of purpose in life? The secular media and culture try to persuade you that you must be master of your own life. You are not, they say, to leave your future to "fate" or some force outside of yourself. If you allow someone else to define your purpose, they argue — whether parent, spouse, boss, or any authority figure — you make it impossible to live to your fullest potential, to fulfill your life's aim. In fact, some claim that if you do not envision your own life and begin to pursue it yourself, you leave your life to chance, to randomness and chaos.

Do you see the meaninglessness in an existence devoid of God's call on your life? It is like the void Solomon spoke about: "So I hated life, because the work that is done under the sun was grievous to me. All of it is meaningless, a chasing after the wind" (Ecclesiastes 2:17). For Christians, however, "it is the Lord's purpose that prevails" (Proverbs 19:21). He provides us with meaning and a mission. He is the Master of our destinies.

Without an understanding *of God's* call on my life, my existence is unfulfilled, random, and chaotic. Jesus came so we may have life and have it to the full (John 10:10)! A self-directed life can never have life to the full. Only Jesus can bring it!

When God your Creator knit you together in your mother's womb, He built a mission into your life— He ordained you and called you to carry out His purpose. As a Christian, you were bought at a price. You should therefore honor God with your life (1 Corinthians 6:20).

You may have already seen the three circles that represent ways we can pattern our lives:[2]

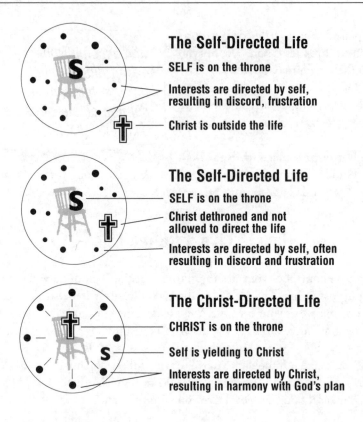

The Self-Directed Life

— SELF is on the throne

— Interests are directed by self,
resulting in discord, frustration

— Christ is outside the life

The Self-Directed Life

— SELF is on the throne

— Christ dethroned and not
allowed to direct the life

— Interests are directed by self, often
resulting in discord and frustration

The Christ-Directed Life

— CHRIST is on the throne

— Self is yielding to Christ

— Interests are directed by Christ,
resulting in harmony with God's plan

The first circle describes the "natural person." God is not a part of these people's lives. They are lord of their own lives and they are in control. In 1 Corinthians 2:14, Paul describes them: "The man without the Spirit does not accept the things that come from the Spirit of God, for they are foolishness to him, and he cannot understand them, because they are spiritually discerned."

The second circle describes the "carnal" or "worldly" person. God appears to be part of their lives, but He is just another of the many things that they try to control. Maybe they go to church, do some good things, and read their Bibles. But *they* are still in control of their lives. Paul says about them,

> *I could not address you as spiritual but as worldly — mere infants in Christ. I gave you milk, not solid food, for you were not ready for it. Indeed you are still not ready. You are still worldly. (1 Corinthians 3:1-3)*

Secular philosophies and principles make sense if you are living in one of the first two circles, but not if you are living in the third circle.

The third circle describes a "spiritual" person. God is not just *part* of their lives, He is their life. They have given the throne over to Him. Spiritual people allow God to direct their lives; they know He has a purpose and plan for them (1 Corinthians 2:15-16; 3:9-16). This is what it means to live as a *called person*.

> *When God your Creator knit you together in your mother's womb, He built a mission into your life — He ordained you and called you to carry out His purpose.*

Let me be clear. It makes sense for secular people who live their own lives in one of the first two circles to want to map out their own vision and purpose in life. What does *not* make sense is for Christians to live this way! Far too many do. They don't recognize God's call on their life because *they* are in control of it.

Only when they surrender, relinquish, resign, yield their life to Him can they really receive life — life to the full — life with a purpose.

Heart to Heart

1. How were you called to be a small group leader? How was it a gift of God's grace?

2. How will you be a good steward of the calling that God has given you? What will you do to be sure you are being a good steward of the group?

3. What really brings fulfillment to your life? Try thinking of the question this way: If you showed up at your own funeral, what would you want people to be saying about you?

Chapter Five

Head and Heart

Sometimes David's actions did not make sense intellectually. Like letting Saul live when he had the opportunity to take his life, even though Saul was tracking David, trying to kill him. Like mourning and weeping over the death of Saul, his enemy. Like allowing Shimeal to curse David and throw stones and dirt on him as he walked along the road (2 Samuel 16:5-14). David didn't manage his kingdom with lots of systems and programs and controls. He led the people with love and a shepherd's heart. He led out of a heart of compassion. Love, not head knowledge, most characterized his leadership.

The Written Word and the Living Word

Knowledge of the written Word of God is essential for living and growing in the Christian life. When the apostle Paul wrote to his young protégé, Timothy, he reminded him of how Timothy had known from infancy the Holy Scriptures, "which are able to make you wise for salvation in Christ Jesus" (2 Timothy 3:15). Paul then reiterated the importance of knowing the Bible: "All Scripture is God-breathed and is useful for teaching, rebuking, correcting, and training in righteousness, so that the man of God may be thoroughly equipped for every good work" (2 Timothy 3:16).

> *Knowledge of the written Word of God is essential for living and growing in the Christian life.*

Before any "good work" can begin, we must equip ourselves by studying the Scriptures.

The Bible links the written Word, Scripture, with the Living Word, Jesus. John wrote about Jesus, "The Word became flesh and made his dwelling among us" (John 1:14). God came to His people as one of us. He came in the ordinary and mundane. He was born in a stable and raised in a wood shop. He spent most of His adult life in the streets talking to ordinary people, poor people, sinners.

> *The Scriptures must move beyond head knowledge; it must be lived out in action.*

"What if God was one of us? Just a slob like one of us?" asked Joan Osborne in a popular song. He was! And the religious teachers and leaders of His day missed what God was up to. Jesus did not fit their expectations or systematic theology. He did not astound them with his head knowledge, even though He had it. He did not astonish them with eloquent speech, although He certainly could have. To them, He was too common to be God.

If these teachers and leaders had really known God, they would have known that Jesus was sent from Him. They would have known from His heart. As it was, all they could see and understand were his outward appearances, which did not look very much like the Son of God to them. They were so hung up on their traditions, rules, and teachings that they missed what they were supposed to be teaching about.

And thus, Jesus told them,

> *You nullify the word of God for the sake of your tradition. You hypocrites! Isaiah was right when he prophesied about you: "These people honor me with their lips, but their hearts are far from me. They worship me in vain; their teachings are but rules taught by men." (Matthew 15:6-9)*

Once, when He was answering the Jewish leaders' allegations and insults, Jesus told them, "You diligently study the Scriptures because you think that by them you possess eternal life. These are the Scriptures that testify about me, yet you refuse to come to me to have life" (John 5:39-40).

These educated men knew the written word backwards and forwards. If they were alive today, most churches would make them Bible study leaders in an instant — that is, if they were not already preachers! But they did not know the Living Word at all.

In our lives and in our small groups, the Word must take flesh! The Scriptures must move beyond head knowledge; it must be lived out in action.

The Living Word, Jesus, must be more than just a name we use; we must live our lives so that He lives in and through us.

Education and Discipleship

Some churches operate as if the number of classes attended, sermons heard, or Sunday school lessons taught is the measurement of a "good Christian." Education itself is not our goal, but only a means to the goal. When we view education as the goal, we produce a crippled, compartmentalized Christianity that doesn't get out into the world where it is desperately needed.

Rewarding people with Sunday school pins for attendance must have seemed like a great idea at the time, but it communicated that the really strong Christians were the ones who never missed a meeting. Besides the obvious problem of promoting a works righteousness, this also gave the church a "meeting mentality." Jesus didn't die for a meeting. He died so that we might have *life!* I think that one of my college professors had it right when he said, "The church is strongest when the building is empty." We must get out of our buildings and out of our living rooms and into the places where non-Christians live and play and just hang out. We must be willing to meet people where they live, as Jesus did.

> *Living as a disciple means more than sitting in a classroom on Sunday morning or in a living room on Tuesday night.*

A meeting mentality leads to an event-driven understanding of church. Christian education becomes an event to attend, but discipleship is an ongoing, lifelong process. The most important thing is not where you *are*, but where you are *going* — and that you continue to head in that direction. That direction is Christlikeness.

Discipleship is "being transformed into his likeness" (2 Corinthians 3:18). This transformation is internal, not external, as revealed in Romans 12:2: "Do not conform any longer to the pattern of this world [external], but be transformed by the renewing of your mind [internal]." Unfortunately, many people in churches and small groups settle for an "imitation transformation," that is, external changes such as knowledge, position and titles, reputation, or attention.

Over time, the church has redefined discipleship into scholarship, Christianity into Churchianity. Living as a disciple means more than sitting in a classroom on Sunday morning or in a living room on Tuesday night. Discipleship is a 24-7, everyday-for-the-rest-of-your-life pursuit empowered by the Holy Spirit.

Dead Faith Versus Power

Jim Cymbala talks about the absurdity of "circling the wagons, busying ourselves with Bible studies among our own kind. There is no demonstration of God's power because we have closed ourselves off from the *need* for such demonstration."[1]

This kind of group is dead because all it has is faith without works. Many such groups died a long time ago, but no one realized it. The people involved just kept meeting as if the group was still alive, but all that existed, in reality, was a cold, stiff corpse. These groups meet weekly; they do studies from Bible study guides; they pray for one another's physical health. But that's it. Like the Dead Sea, there is no outflow of life from the group. There is no demonstration of Spirit's power through outreach and evangelism. Many groups go for years in this kind of lack of awareness or denial.

Another category of dead small groups are those that were never alive in the first place. Our small group ministry assistant Carl describes these groups as mannequins. They were not created with the intention of being living, growing organisms. They study the Word only for knowledge, not to put it into practice. They are "all dressed up with no place to go"! I've visited with mannequin groups; their leaders cannot understand why they need to invite new people into their groups or develop an intern. These groups had not been founded with the expectation of being more than "Bible studies," so they were, as Carl would put it, mannequins, which look good on the outside, but have no life inside.

> *Small groups that are truly alive and growing are groups that are making a real difference in people's lives.*

To understand what a dead group looks like, you have to know the vital signs of a living group. A living group is *growing*. People are being transformed and the lost are being reached — the group is expanding. A living group is *moving*. It doesn't just *meet* or *congregate*; it is actively involved in something outside itself. A living group has a *heartbeat*. It has a *mission and purpose*. It exists to *do* something other than just feed itself. A living group is *maturing*. It's not just getting older, it's developing into what it was created to become.

Meetings Versus Mission

Small group leaders often ask me, "How can I get people interested in coming to my small group?" My answer: Don't summon them to a meeting.

Invite them to make a difference!

People, especially those who are unchurched, will not leave their homes to go to a "safe and comfortable" small group meeting. Why would they? They already have safe and comfortable! What they *don't* have is the sense of fulfillment and purpose that comes from making a real difference in the world.

Small groups that are truly alive and growing are groups that are making a real difference in people's lives. They don't meet just to "do Bible study;" they gather to transform lives through the application of God's Word and then scatter to *do* what the Word says.

They meet people's true needs, like Jesus did. They are incarnational — bringing God's love and power into people's lives. Members of these small groups see themselves as ministers of reconciliation for a world that needs to be reconnected to God.

Milk Versus Maturity

A small group is like a human body that Paul discussed in Romans 12 and 1 Corinthians 12. In a living body, each part is working. In a living group, each person is growing, moving, and maturing. As I look at people in churches, even those in small groups, I notice that many seem to be just sitting there. They are being fed, but the nutrition isn't being put to use. They keep getting fatter and fatter.

A few months ago, I was talking on the phone with a man who was interested in getting involved in a small group. When I asked what he was looking for in a group, he said he needed to be in a group with an elder from the church or someone else who could answer all of the biblical questions that he and other members might have.

I asked if he was a new Christian.

No, he said, he had grown up in a Christian home, his father was a preacher in another state, and he had been involved in the church for a long time.

I had to bite my lip. I wanted to echo the words of the writer to the Hebrews, who faced the same sort of situation in the people to whom he was trying to minister:

We have much to say about this, but it is hard to explain because you are slow to learn. In fact, though by this time you ought to be teachers, you need someone to teach you the elementary truths of God's word all over again. You need milk, not solid food! Anyone who lives on milk, being still an infant, is not acquainted with the teaching about righteousness.

But solid food is for the mature, who by constant use have trained themselves to distinguish good from evil.

Therefore let us leave the elementary teachings about Christ and go on to maturity. (Hebrews 5:11-6:1)

I didn't go there; the time wasn't right. But this conversation reminded me of many people who insist on having the preachers, teachers, and small group leaders feeding them. They still want their baby bottles, even though they have the teeth for meat!

As leaders, we need to consider whether we are part of the solution or part of the problem. I have talked with many group leaders who are frustrated because members are not growing to maturity even though the leaders keep providing nourishment. What these leaders need to understand is that for people to grow, they need to learn to feed themselves. They need to be putting the Word into practice. They need to start leading and teaching others behind them on the spiritual path.

When my children were babies, from time to time we would intentionally remove something from them to move them from dependence to interdependence. Each one started out naturally with total dependence on Mom.

Over time, we moved each one from Mommy to a baby bottle, but we eventually took away the bottle and moved each one to a sippy cup, and finally to a big boy's or big girl's cup. Sure, there were spills along the way, but they were learning and growing. With each step, our children became less and less dependent on us and more and more able to feed themselves. They were moving toward maturity. Someday, they will do the same for our grandchildren. As spiritual families, we must start moving people from milk to maturity!

> As spiritual families, we must start moving people from milk to maturity.

Apathy Versus Mission and Values

Why are so many people still babes in Christ even though they have been believers for a long time? Why do people stop maturing? Why are groups dying? What's wrong in our small groups and churches? I believe it all boils down to one factor: *Both individuals and small groups do not know, fully understand, or live out any kind of mission, purpose, values, and goals.*

There is a goal to living and maturing in the spiritual life. People who are being taught should some day start teaching others what they are learning.

People who are being led should at some time start leading others. People who are truly being discipled will begin to disciple. It's a natural part of life — or it should be. But far too often, it's not!

A living, powerful small group has a mission, purpose, and goals. A dead group has none of these. A living group lives by a certain set of inherent values. A dead group may have some unstated values, but these values move the group more toward death than life. (For instance, an unstated value in a group may be, "We are a closed clique. We like each other too much to let anyone else in." Or, "This group exists to take care of my own needs for relationship. If *my* needs are not being met, I'm out of here.")

At the church where I minister, the following are the stated values for our small groups. These are the heart and soul of our groups and they are what keep the groups on mission. Note that these are not based on outward appearances, but on the heart. We communicate them regularly to group leadership and members.[2]

- **UPWARD** (connected to God): The group is dependent on God, led by the Holy Spirit, and focused on Jesus. Worship and prayer connect us personally with God and unleash His power to work in and through the group.

- **INWARD** (connecting to each other): A group is a family that cares for one another. Every member of the group is a minister to and with the rest of the group.

- **OUTWARD** (making disciples): The group intentionally demonstrates God's love by members pro-actively inviting and accepting new people, especially non-Christians and church visitors. People meet Christ and accept Him as Lord and Savior in the environment of an authentic, loving small group.

- **FORWARD** (maturing): Believers mature in a small group as they apply God's Word to their lives. Both group times and one-on-one discipleship (mentoring) are used to help individuals grow in their faith.

- **ONWARD** (empowering): Family members (group members) grow up and leave home! Producing and releasing leaders is a natural occurrence in a healthy group.

The last two values, "Forward" and "Onward," are especially important to communicate clearly. When a child grows up physically, but not emotionally or mentally, we usually assume there is a problem. A healthy 40-year-old adult who still lives at home with Mom and Dad is the exception to the rule, and there are usually circumstances behind it. The normal, natural occurrence is for kids to grow up to a certain level of maturity and responsibility and then to leave home and start their own households.

In far too many groups, these values are not being lived out. So the group becomes ingrown, self-absorbed, and stagnant. Groups that live by values that help them focus upward, inward, outward, forward, and onward have real life, life to the full!

Knowledge Versus
Authentic Community and Real Transformation

The goal of a small group is not to become more knowledgeable about Scripture. "Knowledge puffs up" (1 Corinthians 8:1a). *Knowledge* of Scripture — studying and interpreting it in the small group — is a means to the end. The end product is maturity in Christ (Hebrews 6:1), which enables us to love deeply and unconditionally. "Love builds up" (1 Corinthians 8:1b).

"Do not merely listen to the word, and so deceive yourselves. Do what it says" (James 1:22). Studying God's Word without *doing* what it says is the embalming fluid of group life. I can imagine visitors to such a group saying, "Don't they look lifelike?" If they were to hang around long enough, they would never see any real life. Merely listening to the word may deceive the group and others for a short time, but when there is no movement, they are found out for what they are: dead.

The point of studying the Bible in the group is transformation. Too many groups settle for information. They settle for "Christian intellectualism" (a paradox, in my opinion). They even define how "spiritual" a person is by how much he or she knows. From that perspective, the Pharisees were the most spiritual people of Jesus' day!

The Word must become flesh in the group! The "study" of Scripture must be active and alive. It must be dynamic, not static; energetic, not lethargic. Involved in real ministry, not passive or heady. The small group experience must relate to the hands and the heart, and not merely the head.

> *The point of studying the Bible in the group is transformation.*

Jesus' disciples are our best example of a living, powerful small group. They changed the world! As this small group went into the world and multiplied over and over and over again, thousands of people were changed. Because of that group, you and I are Christians today.

Out of My Mind and Into My Car

People are the heart of ministry. I have known that intellectually for a long time. For years I would walk into my office each day and see *things* to do, and start doing them. Five o'clock would roll around and it was time to head home. At the end of the week, month, and year, I looked back and wondered what had happened to all my goals — the goals and purposes I knew God wanted to work through my life. I was frustrated with my ministry and needed to be infused, empowered, and transformed.

God started transforming me one day as I spoke to a friend and mentor on the phone. He gave me encouragement and great tips on how to begin to change my ministry style. One of his ideas reminded me of a line from an '80s song: "Get out of my mind, and into my car." I needed to get out of the realm of the mind — the structure and forms of small group ministry — and into my car where I could get out and meet with people. I started making that change in my ministry right away.

But that was only the beginning. About a week later I attended the 2000 Willow Creek Small Group Conference. The theme was, "Authentic Community . . . Real Transformation." John Ortberg started the conference by talking about "A Transformed Life." He asked two important questions in his session: "What kind of person are we trying to produce in our church?" and "What kind of church are we producing?" The same questions should be asked in our small groups.

External Versus Internal

Dan Webster spoke at the Willow Creek Small Group Conference about "Becoming Authentic Leaders," comparing the external life of the leader with the more essential internal life.

He told the story of Michael Plant, an experienced sailor who set off to sail his boat across the Atlantic Ocean. During the voyage, Plant faced raging storms at sea, but he was an experienced sailor, so naval experts were not worried. Then radio operators lost contact with Plant. Eventually a search party was sent out, and sadly, Plant's sailboat was found, bottom up. This is very unusual, because the keel, a weighted structure extending longitudinally along the center of the underside of the boat, is designed to keep the ship floating right side up. When the searchers found Plant's sailboat, the first thing they noticed was that the keel had broken off.

Webster used this story as a picture of leadership. What is *below* the waterline, he said, is much more critical than everything that is *above* the water. The things you see, like sails, the wheel, the mast, are important to the effectiveness of the boat, but what is below the waterline, what is not seen, is even more crucial.

For leaders, the things above the waterline are the external things: skills, talents, knowledge, strategies, positive mental attitude, and relational abilities, for instance. People who try to lead from the external qualities are performance oriented; they lead by charisma. They are led by and lead by control, position, fear, and politics.

John Maxwell says they are managers rather than leaders. They are maintainers who depend on systems and controls. These people lead from the head and are primarily concerned with effectiveness.

The things below the waterline are character and heart. "Heart and soul" leaders know that their life and their leadership flow from the condition of their hearts. They live by Proverbs 4:23: "Above all else, guard your heart, for it is the wellspring of life." They lead by character and integrity. Their leadership flows from an ongoing intimacy with God. They are "called leaders."

When seeking new leaders for small groups, I prayerfully look at people's hearts to see the good that God is doing in their lives, and then I ask them to consider leading a group. Many times the answer will be, "No, I don't feel like I *know* enough about the Bible yet" or "I'm not ready yet; I don't have the skills or abilities" or "No, I am too shy to be a leader." Our society has told them that the stuff above the waterline is really important, and as a result, some of the best potential leaders with the most Godly hearts won't step up to lead.

Foolishness Versus Wisdom

In today's church, we are desperate for authentic leaders. Authentic small group leaders facilitate and shepherd out of the power of the Holy Spirit; they use their God-given gifts to impact the world. They are involved in people's lives on a common spiritual journey together. They are disciple makers, mentors, developers, and reproducers. They love to give ministry away to others.

Authentic small group leaders are not necessarily super-intelligent; they are not necessarily the ones in the group who know the most about the Bible or who have the highest IQ. Paul says, "it is required that those who have been given a trust must prove *faithful*" (1 Corinthians 4:2, my emphasis). Faithfulness, not intelligence, skill, or personality, is what is required. In fact, Paul said, "Do not be deceived. If any one of you thinks he is wise by the standards of this age [conforming to the external patterns of the world], he should become a 'fool' so that he may become wise. For the wisdom of the world is foolishness in God's sight" (1 Corinthians 3:18-19). The best small group leaders know one thing for sure: they do not know it all, but they do have a heart after God. They are willing to listen and learn from others, especially God.

Unfortunately, a lot of small group leadership is really boasting: "See how much I know? Just ask me a question, and I'll give you the answer." That is foolishness in God's sight! The *worst* small group leaders are the ones that make the group dependent on them. They need to hear, "Our small group leader is really good. He knows so much about the Bible. I learn so much from him!" That too is foolishness. "No more boasting about men," Paul insists (1 Corinthians 3:21).

Let's say you are looking for a leader in training (intern) for your group. What characteristics will you look for? Usually, in our conformity to the pattern of this world, we look at the external things. The biggie is knowledge. "If they don't know enough, they can't lead a small group," we assert. Why? If you really want "puffed-up" leaders, then

Authentic small group leaders are disciple makers, mentors, developers, and reproducers.

knowledge is the true test. If you want leaders after God's own heart, then love is the true test. So you must look below the surface at the internal qualities — the heart and soul qualities — first.

Christ's love compels true leadership. If you are looking for a leader, look for a person who has love before you look for a person who has knowledge. That is the kind of person who will *build up* a group.

A small group after God's own heart must be connected intimately and mightily to God through prayer and worship. God's love and power brings real, abundant, transformational life to the group.

Heart to Heart

1. How would you define *discipleship*? What is it? What is it not? What do you think your role is in making disciples?

2. As a spiritual leader, how, specifically, will you help people grow in their faith? Who should you be feeding? Who should you be teaching to feed themselves? Who should be learning to feed others?

3. Read Luke 6:31. How would you put this verse into action in your group?

4. In what areas do you need to be transformed to become a leader guided by love rather than knowledge?

Chapter Six

A Heart of
Worship and Prayer

When the Ark was brought into Jerusalem (2 Samuel 6:12-22); David understood that it was an event worth rejoicing over. Rejoice he did, dancing and leaping in the streets with his party clothes on. Some folks in town — even his wife — were pretty ashamed of his actions. After all, he was a man of distinction, the leader of his country, and a religious man. This was, well, undignified. But God was doing something that deserved praise, honor, and worship without reserve. So David rejoiced with all his might, regardless of what others' thoughts. God was pleased with his praise. It showed, once again, that David was a man after God's own heart.

Leaders after God's heart will, like David, yearn to worship God. Worship is part of our spiritual DNA.

Does Worship Belong in Small Groups?

Worship is an essential part of the Christian's life, both individually and corporately. But does worship belong in small groups? That is like asking, does a heart belong in the human body? Does an operating system belong on a computer? Does peanut butter belong in a PBJ sandwich? Does chocolate belong in a chocolate-chip cookie?

Worship makes a small group run. It's what holds it together. It's what makes a sweet aroma, pleasing to God. It has been that way since the beginning of the church.

Jesus and His disciples worshiped together in the Upper Room at the Last Supper (Luke 14:26). The believers praised God together when Peter and John were released from prison, and "the place where they were meeting was shaken" (Acts 4:23-31).

On another occasion, "about midnight, Paul and Silas were praying and singing hymns to God, and the other prisoners were listening to them. Suddenly there was such a violent earthquake that the foundations of the prison were shaken" (Acts 16:25-26). This is a great illustration of "cell worship"!

When God's people gather together, it is natural for them to worship. They do not necessarily have to dance and leap in the streets like David. They do not even have to sing. *How* they worship God is not as important as the fact that they choose to worship Him. When they do, God shakes things up!

Why Don't We Worship More in Small Groups?

Worship belongs in small groups, but many factors keep groups from entering into it:

- *Intellectualism.* When *knowledge* of the Bible is the main objective, God gets crowded out. *Agendaitus* is the problem. The group simply does not have time in their tight schedule for worship and meaningful prayer.

- *Self-Centeredness.* The question must be asked, "For whom does this group exist?" If the answer is "me, my family, and our needs," it's time to go back to the beginning and discuss purpose and mission.

- *Never Thought of It.* Many existing, long-standing groups simply never connect "worship" with "small group." Worship has never been held up as small group value so they don't practice it.

- *No True Experience in Worship.* Some group members may have not experienced real worship, so they don't look for it or miss it in the group.

- *A View that Worship and Evangelism Are Diametrically Opposed.* This is not true. While pre-Christians may not be able to enter into worship as completely as a fully devoted follower of Christ, just being in the room with sincere people who are praising God — and seeing God move in response — will draw a person to God. Worship changes people. Just like it changed the Philippian jailer and his family!

• *Spiritual Warfare.* Satan does whatever he can to prevent us from spending time with God. He hates it when we come together to worship God in spirit and in truth.

What is a group where God is not present? Secular. Truly transformational small groups are groups that focus on God, His will, His Word, and His ways. When we worship, we welcome God into our presence.

What God Does When Groups Worship

In worship we ascribe *worth* to God. We give Him praise for who He is rather than what He has done. We acknowledge and affirm His character, His power, and His sovereignty. A small group yielded to God will naturally spend time in worship and prayer. When they do, God will pour His love and power into the group. People grow in Christlikeness and life balance as they come close to God through worship and prayer. Their relationship with God develops as they

> *When we worship, we welcome God into our presence.*

spend time with Him individually, in a small group, and corporately. As Calvin Coolidge put it, "It is only when men begin to worship that they begin to grow." The result of spending time with God as a group through worship and prayer is a group's ability to minister *with* each other to others as the overflow of their hearts pours into the lives around them.

Worship, therefore, has a threefold purpose in the small group.

First, it pleases God. He is *worthy* of our worship! As God's children, we need to enter into God's *presence.* At the end of this life, we as Christians will spend the rest of eternity in the presence of God worshiping and praising Him (see Revelation 4:8-11). Now, we have the opportunity to practice for eternity!

Second, it bolsters spiritual growth in individuals. Worship is essential to life! Everyone chooses to worship *something.* Many people chase after things that do not ultimately bring life and joy and peace. As we give our lives to God and begin to live according to His will, we focus our lives on Him. This gives us a higher *purpose* in life.

Third, it empowers the group to reach out. God has given us a mission and the power to accomplish it. That power comes as we yield ourselves totally to Him in worship.

We need to understand that worship is more than just a nice thing to do. We have been created to worship God, so when we fail to do so, we live outside of His will. Romans 1:21 says, "For although they knew God, they neither glorified him as God nor gave thanks to him, but their thinking became futile and their foolish hearts were darkened." The passage goes on to say that these people exchanged true worship for God for idolatry. Failing to worship leads us to sin (Romans 1:22-32).

> *Prayer and worship must start in the personal life of the leaders, and then flow into the group.*

Small group dynamics, like asking good questions or listening effectively, are important. None are as important as the dynamics of prayer and worship. Most dynamics have to do with horizontal relationships; that is, relationships between two or more people, but prayer and worship bring into the group the vertical relationship, the primary relationship between God and us.

Prayer and worship must start in the personal life of the leaders, and then flow into the group. Prayer and worship invite God's presence, purpose, and power into the group.

God's Presence

Godly leaders have hearts that beat with David's in Psalm 42: "As the deer pants for streams of water, so my soul pants for you, O God. My soul thirsts for God, for the living God. When can I go and meet with God?" Leaders seek a quiet time of communion with God daily. It is their time to go and meet with God to allow Him to be Lord of their life.

These leaders also have the heart of Mary, the sister of Martha and Lazarus, and a dear friend of Jesus'. Mary is mentioned just three times in the gospels; in two of these instances, as she sought to do something special for Jesus, her actions were misunderstood. All three of these times we find Mary at Jesus' feet.

In Luke 10, Mary found her blessing at his feet. Remember the story of Mary and Martha? Jesus had come to their home and Martha was busy in the kitchen. Meanwhile Mary sat at Jesus' feet, listening to him speak. Martha was upset and asked Jesus to get Mary to help work. Jesus mildly rebuked Martha for her words, but he blessed Mary for choosing what was better: a relationship with Jesus.

In John 11, Mary brought her burdens to Jesus' feet. Her brother Lazarus had died, and now Jesus had come, four days later. The Scripture says that Mary ran to Jesus and fell at his feet, crying. Moved by her sorrow, Jesus wept too.

And in John 12, Mary gave her best at Jesus' feet. Mary walked into a party being held in Jesus' honor holding a pint of expensive perfume. It was imported from India in carefully sealed alabaster jars to preserve the fragrance.

An average person would save for a lifetime to buy a pound of the ointment and then only use it at his or her burial.

Mary broke the jar, pouring out the perfume onto Jesus' feet, and then wiped them with her hair. Some of those present began to attack Mary for her extravagant gift, but Jesus rebuked them and praised Mary. She understood that the most important thing in life is to be in the presence of the Lord. A relationship with Him is more important than anything else.

One day in August a few years ago, I opened my journal to my last entry: April 22. I could hardly believe my eyes. It had been four months since my last "real" quiet time. Oh, I had prayed. Even daily. But my prayer times were sporadic, and they rarely, if ever, included a time just to be quiet before God, listening for His still, small voice.

I had plenty of excuses. I had been busy with important things . . . my ministry and my family. So busy that my time with God got crowded out. I know one thing for sure: Satan loves it when I'm that busy!

Those four months seemed dry as dust. My relationships at home were rocky. My ministry was exhausting. There was little power or purpose in my days and weeks. I needed to experience being present with God again. I opened my Bible to the place where I had left off four months before: Psalm 42. When I read the first few verses, I knew that God had a message for me: "As the deer pants for streams of water, so my soul pants for you, O God. My soul thirsts for God, for the living God. When can I go and meet with God?"

> *As small group leaders, we sometimes get so busy being concerned with other's spiritual lives that our own relationship with God suffers.*

As small group leaders, we sometimes get so busy being concerned with other's spiritual lives that our own relationship with God suffers. We must regularly remind ourselves that life is about relationship *with* God, not religious activity *for* Him. As shepherds of God's flocks, we must be in touch with our Guide, our Good Shepherd, our Master. Without His direction, we may be leading His flocks into danger.

Even if our groups seem to be going well, without communion with God it is pointless. If we are not connected to God, what does it matter how many people come to our group or how many books of the Bible we study together? I have led groups where after the meeting people have said things like, "Wasn't that dessert scrumptious?" or "What a great group. I really like the people here!" or even "Wasn't that a great study Mike led?" Those comments are nice, but they do not define a successful meeting or group. When people leave saying things like, "Isn't God good? He really touched my life tonight . . ." then I know it was a victory.

God's Purpose

When Mary entered the room with her alabaster jar, she didn't come to see other people, she came to worship Jesus. Like King David, she didn't care what others might say about her. She was there for one reason — to give Jesus a gift before He died. He had saved her from her past. Now she was going to offer Him a gift of love. She seized the moment.

Mary had spent time with Jesus. She had sat at His feet and listened to Him. Even though His disciples had followed Jesus for three years, Mary may have understood Jesus better than they did. Jesus had told them several times that He would die and then be raised again, but they still weren't ready for His death. But Mary knew. She came to this dinner prepared with ointment to anoint His body for burial.

She worshipped Him with holy abandonment. The only way we can learn to worship like this is if we've been through hardship. We can't learn it from a sermon, a class, or even a small group. We learn it by going through humbling circumstances in life and realizing our need for Him. Only His power can bring us to worship Him with holy abandonment.

Worshipping Jesus with holy abandonment changes all of our values. The perfume Mary brought was worth a year's wages. It was precious to her. She made a personal sacrifice to give this gift to Jesus.

> *God wants us to surrender our lives to Him ... not just commit, but surrender.*

God wants us to surrender our lives to Him . . . not just commit, but surrender. We commit to church membership. We commit to a mortgage. We commit to a loan payment. We make commitments all the time, but *we're* still in control. God wants to be the only one in control of our lives; when we surrender to Him, our lives are blessed beyond measure.

Mary surrendered all she was and all she had for Jesus. She did what she could for Him. She gave Him her very best. Mary didn't just *open* the jar. She *broke* it. When you open a jar or bottle, you can control how the contents come out. You can put the top back on to save some for another time. When the jar is broken, the contents just flow out. You can't control it. You can't stop it.

Most of us have been opened; we say things like "God has really opened my heart to Him" or "I have made myself open to God's Spirit." Very few of us have been truly broken by the Holy Spirit! Broken emotionally. Broken of some sin or sinful lifestyle. Broken in such a way that we understand that only God can put the pieces back together. Broken as David was after his sin with Bathsheba (2 Samuel 11-12). Broken to the point where God can create in you a pure heart and renew a steadfast spirit within you (Psalm 51:10), where He can restore to you the joy of His salvation (Psalm 51:12).

When we too are broken, our worship flows out. Nothing gets in the way. Too often I have held back the contents of my alabaster jar, afraid to come broken before God. What would others think? What if I lost control? What if I couldn't put the pieces back together?

Mary wasn't worried about putting the pieces back together. Mary didn't hold anything back from Jesus. She broke the jar and let it all flow out to her Savior.

God's Purpose: Revival

When we come to God and worship Him with holy abandonment, we avail ourselves to His purpose. He can work through our lives, our groups, and our churches. He can bring revival!

We are in great need of revival in America all across the world. Some believe small groups are the answer. They aren't. Small groups have no more chance of initiating revival than a fireplace has of starting a fire. No programs, methods, philosophies, or forms can bring about what only God can do. Regardless of how biblically sound, culturally relevant, and structurally effective they are, small groups themselves do not bring rebirth.

Even the best small group leader cannot bring revival. No amount of training, spiritual giftedness, or holy passion will bring it about. Only God creates, initiates, and orchestrates revival. Only God.

Jesus told His followers that He could do nothing on His own, but only by the Father's initiation.[1] If God's Son worked from this viewpoint, how can we claim that our methods, models, and ministries can do anything? We must realize that small groups are not the answer. A new model is not the answer. House churches are not the answer. The cell church is not the answer. Better leadership training is not the answer. This book is not the answer.

Jesus is the answer. We can do *nothing* apart from God. The Holy Spirit is our real leader. Small groups can be the fireplace where the fire starts, but let's get rid of the notion that small groups *are* the fire — or even the match.

As Henry Blackaby and Claude King point out, God is always at work (cf. John 5:17). All we need to do is discover where he is already at work and join him in that work. Or, as Rick Warren has illustrated in *The Purpose Driven Church*, a surfer does not try to create waves. He waits for the wave that God provides, and then rides it for all it's worth. God will

> *Regardless of how biblically sound, culturally relevant, and structurally effective they are, small groups themselves do not bring rebirth.*

provide the waves that will bring revival. When He does, be ready with your surfboard!

God's Purpose: Transformation

How can small groups become fireplaces in which God can start some fires? It must start with these small clusters of God's people falling to their knees in prayer, seeking God, accepting the love relationship He has extended to us, asking Him to move in our midst, and watching as He begins to work. *Then*, we can begin to join Him in the work. As we experience our Father's unconditional love, we can begin to extend that same love to others. Then our groups will begin bearing much fruit, fruit that will last, and God's Kingdom will be expanded because of the fresh winds of revival that He has brought.

> *God will provide the waves that will bring revival.*

If people's lives are changed, it will be because God is transforming them from the inside out. If people are reached with the gospel, it will be because the Holy Spirit is convicting them and changing their hearts. If people are healed, it will be because the Great Physician is touching them. The amazing thing is that God chooses to use us in the process of carrying out His purpose of transforming lives — if we are available to Him to use us.

God's Power

In Jesus' day, it was not socially acceptable for a woman to let down her hair in public. It was the sign of a harlot. A woman's hair was her glory (1 Corinthians 11:15). When Mary let down her hair to wipe Jesus' feet, she surrendered her glory to the Lord. It was a gift of love and devotion that brought a sweet fragrance to the whole house.

To worship God, we may need to let down our hair. We may have to do what is socially unacceptable, as David did when he danced before the Lord in Jerusalem.

Mary did not do anything spectacular. She was an ordinary person who did what to her was an ordinary thing. Jesus considered her gift extraordinary! He was so moved by her selfless act that He said it would be remembered in all future generations.

The old saying is true: God uses ordinary people to do extraordinary things. His power is best displayed through weak vessels (like you and me) but only when we are attached to the Vine, only when we are in communion with God.

Leaders Pray

Before I start inviting people to a new group, I begin praying — for me as a leader, for the group as a whole, and for the individuals who will be invited to the group. I pray for people by name, especially those who are not believers, and I ask God to begin working in their hearts. When the group begins to meet, I take time each day to pray for each person in the group. Beyond that, I take time each day to pray especially for one or two individuals in the group. For instance, if there are ten people in the group, I write two people's names on each of the weekdays of my calendar in a given week. I consider it part of my responsibility as a leader to hold them up to my Father in prayer every day. I encourage other members to do the same.

Groups Pray

I give special attention to prayer in meetings. I remind participants that prayer is more than just asking God for things. It is communicating our feelings and thoughts to Him. I try to steer the group away from surface-level requests: Aunt Mary's sick cat, the missionaries in Botswana, a friend of a cousin whose mother is having her appendix removed. Those may be legitimate things to pray for, but group prayer has a particular purpose and should center on the group and its outreach.

Keep your group prayer time creative. For instance, focus prayer times on specific needs or topics. Take a night and pray only for families or friends at work, or spend an evening praising God for His grace or His power; use your prayer time to confess sins to God and to one another (James 5:16) — but don't do this last one with first-time guests present!

> *I consider it part of my responsibility as a leader to hold my group members up to my Father in prayer every day.*

Group Members Pray for One Another

In the group, care and prayer for one another go hand in hand. The New Testament shows a church that naturally cared for and ministered to one another. Small groups are places where everyone is involved in ministering to one another, not where one person serves and cares for everyone else. They are places where everyone has an opportunity to use the spiritual gifts God has given them.

Within the first few weeks of a new group, I pass out index cards and have everyone write their name and contact information on one side and the things they would like regular prayer for on the other side. At the end of the meeting, we put the names in a hat and everyone draws a card. They meet with that person after the meeting to talk, share other prayer requests, minister to and pray for each other. (This means each person will meet with two different people after the end of the meeting — the person they are praying for and the one that is praying for them.) They should continue to pray for that person every day as well as contact them to encourage, pray out loud for, and build accountability with their partner.

Prayer Produces Growth

For my four young children, growth is natural. As long as their mom and I provide the right conditions — good nutrition, a safe environment, and opportunity for exercise — their growth will be automatic. Lack of growth would mean that something is terribly wrong.

The early church grew and grew and grew. Growth was natural for them because the conditions for growth were right. They were the *body* of Christ, and that body was, and is, made to grow. The Book of Acts shows what those conditions were. Acts 2:42-47 summarizes the rest of the book; they were a learning, worshipping, praying, sharing, unselfish church. "And the Lord added to their number daily those who were being saved."

It's fascinating to see how often prayer is mentioned in Acts. The disciples joined together constantly in prayer (Acts 1:14). In fact, there was a regular time of prayer at 3:00 P.M. (Acts 3:1). Luke records the powerful prayer of the believers and reports that the place where they were meeting was shaken and that believers began to preach the word of God boldly (Acts 4:23-31). And Paul and Silas prayed and sang hymns to God in prison (Acts 16:26).

The largest church in the world, Yoido Full Gospel Church (YFGC) in Seoul, Korea, is a great example of a church that believes in the power of prayer. David Yonggi Cho, the senior minister of that church, wrote a book in 1984, when the church was averaging 12,000 new converts a month. The book was titled, *Prayer: Key to Revival.*

Karen Hurston grew up at YFGC. She says there are five elements that have made their cell system bring growth and retention: (1) homogeneous groups, (2) priority to prayer and God's Word, (3) prayer visits by group leaders to participants and unbelievers, (4) a modeling pastoral staff, and (5) leaders who prayerfully and intentionally set significant goals for themselves.[2] For this church, prayer and "success" have gone hand-in-hand.

Hurston says that the typical small group leader prays for an hour a day, more than half of them attend one all-night prayer meeting each week, many fast for specific unbelievers to come to a saving relationship with Christ, and most make three to five prayer visits to members' homes each week.[3] These leaders are committed to their groups and committed to God in prayer! Some of their small groups spend as much as two-thirds of their meeting time in prayer.

A staff pastor at this church said, "More important than all the growth-producing practices at our church is the presence and reality of spiritual empowerment. As we join with God in prayer for ourselves and for others, He gives us *His* power, wisdom, and strength." You might have the most creative ideas, develop the most innovative strategies, lead the most dynamic meetings, and plan the most exciting outreach events, but it will be *prayer* that makes the biggest difference in your group!

In *Reap the Harvest,* Joel Comiskey reports on his research of some of the most successful cell churches around the world; he says the number one reason these churches are fruitful is their dependence on Jesus through prayer. Many pastors visit these churches and become enamored with their systems, Comiskey says. But the power is not in the model; it's in their dependence on God through prayer. Several people from the International Charismatic Mission in Bogotá, Colombia, have said, "Copying our system without the power of the Spirit of God is like buying a car without a motor."[4]

When we pray, we are taking things out of our own hands and putting them into God's hands. It is God's power, not our own strength, that will build His church.

Prayer Unleashes God's Power

Right after Heidi and I got married, we moved into a forty-unit apartment building. We wanted to start a small group to reach out to the unbelievers who lived there, but we had no idea how to start one. So I asked Glen, a minister at the church we attended, how we should proceed.

"I don't think you should do a group yet," he said. "Build some friendships with the people first, pray for the people there, and then ask some of those friends to a small group when the time seems right."

> It is God's power, not our own strength, that will build His church.

"But how will we know when the time is right?" I asked.

"I don't know. Just pray. The Holy Spirit will let you know," he said.

That wasn't exactly the answer I was looking for. My pragmatic nature wanted a specific date and time and a 10-point list of how to's. But we did what Glen suggested — making friends, praying, looking for the Spirit to move. We found out where people liked to hang out, and hung out with them. We looked for opportunities to build friendships as we rode the elevator, did laundry, and helped people who were moving in. We went to various parties and game nights at others' apartments. We drank our cokes while they drank their beers — and we found we got better at the games as the night progressed! We asked them about themselves, listened to them, loved them, and did not judge them. But we lived as Christians before them.

A year and a half later we were still befriending, praying, and watching. I thought Glen was crazy. We wondered if the Holy Spirit would ever "let us know." Then one evening Sherry, the apartment building manager, stopped me. She told me that Sigma, who lived in the building with her boyfriend, Vic, had been approached by a member of a cult and invited to attend a Bible study with them. Sherry asked me to talk to Sigma about this cult.

Sigma and about six other people from our building were sitting around a table by the swimming pool. I told Sigma what I knew and answered her questions. In the midst of our conversation, a longhaired guy who wore black AC/DC T-shirts and sometimes smelled like marijuana said, "Why don't we just start our own Bible study here?"

Someone else chimed in, "Yeah, we could meet at different people's apartments each week. We could invite other people from the building too!"

Then Sherry looked at me and said, "This sounds great, but we need someone who knows about the Bible to teach . . . Mike would you lead it?"

I said yes and then sat back in my chair and let them plan the whole thing.

> *Never forget that "your" small group is God's endeavor.*

A week later we started a study on the basics of Christianity. First Vic came to Christ. I baptized him in the apartment building's swimming pool early one Sunday morning, waking up half the building when Vic let out a whoop as he entered the cold water. Sigma gave her life to Christ later on. Eventually everyone in that group turned their lives over to Jesus, some after we had moved away from the building.

Never forget that "your" small group is *God's* endeavor, for which we as leaders have the privilege of being His ambassadors. Nothing of real significance is ever accomplished in a small group apart from God's leading and power. If we will allow Him to work, He will surprise us every time!

The Lord's arm is not too short! (Numbers 11:21-23). His grace and strength are sufficient for all of our needs. "His divine power has given us everything we need for life and godliness" (1 Peter 1:3).

The greatest Christian leaders have been people with hearts fixed on God and disciplined spiritual lives. Many have set aside a specific time and place to spend with God in personal worship and prayer each day. They have practiced specific spiritual practices to draw them close to God.

As small group leaders who want to be a people after God's own heart, we too must become disciplined in our desire to know God. We cannot lead our groups where we are not residing ourselves. We need a true hunger and thirst for God, which grows out of a deep understanding of and sincere appreciation for Him, His mercy, His holiness, and every part of His nature.

When we understand that, we will know what it means to long for God as a deer pants for water, as the woman at the well thirsted for Living Water, as the crowd hungered for the Bread of Life, as Mary yearned to spend time at Jesus' feet, and as David desired to praise God with all His heart, even with leaping and dancing. Then God will be able to use us as He did them, to reconcile a lost world to Himself.

Heart to Heart

1. Why are worship and prayer important elements of a Christian leader's life? How do you as an individual worship and pray?

2. What do prayer and worship accomplish in a small group? Why are they so vital?

3. How will you make worship and prayer stronger disciplines in your life?

Chapter Seven

A Heart of Reconciliation

God's mercy overflowed from David's heart. Because of God's graciousness to him, David extended forgiveness time and time again. He left judgment in God's hands and chose to seek reconciliation with those who tried to harm him. Psalm 51, which David wrote after being confronted about his adultery with Bathsheba, is a song of confession, contrition, and repentance, but also one of reconciliation between himself and God.

We do not usually think of David as an evangelist. However, in 1 Chronicles 16:23-24, David wrote, "Sing to the Lord, all the earth; proclaim his salvation day after day. Declare his glory among the nations, his marvelous deeds among all peoples." David was encouraging the people, as witnesses of God's power and grace, to tell others about Him. That is our call today.

David's experience of being reconciled to God, even though he did not deserve it, fed his desire to want to proclaim God's salvation to all people. His compassion for people who did not know God was not just a concept or theory; it was a day-to-day lifestyle, a matter of the heart.

I Am a Child of God

I want you to take time and ponder something. As you read the next paragraph, don't just read over it and continue on. Think about each sentence. Meditate on this concept. Consider what it means to your life.

As a Christian, you are a child of God. When you gave your life to Him, He adopted you as His own son or daughter. He has given you all the rights of being His child. Everything you need, really need, is available to you for the asking. Of all His attributes as a Father, the one that stands out most is His love for you . . . unconditional love. He is a "Daddy" you can depend on. He has made you a partner and a co-laborer with Him in the family business.

Take time, if you haven't already, to pray about your response to these thoughts.

When I think and pray about this, it leads me to worship God. I know I don't deserve to be His son and to have all the privileges that go with it; somehow, He loves me as His own child. It doesn't end there! As His child, He has made me a part of the family enterprise, the business of reaching all His lost children to reconcile and redeem them as His own.

> *Therefore, if anyone is in Christ, he is a new creation; the old has gone, the new has come! All this is from God, who reconciled us to himself through Christ and gave us the ministry of reconciliation: that God was reconciling the world to himself in Christ, not counting men's sins against them. And he has committed to us the message of reconciliation. We are therefore Christ's ambassadors, as though God were making his appeal through us. We implore you on Christ's behalf: Be reconciled to God. (2 Corinthians 5:17-20)*

We have a name for God's family: the church. The family business is the mission of the church: to reconcile people to the Father and to restore their lives to God's original design for them. God gave us two special gifts: the gift of community with Him through Jesus and the gift of community to share with one another as believers. We are to proclaim what we have seen and heard about Jesus, who made all this possible, to others so that they may have community with God and us (1 John 1:2-3).

God's Heart of Reconciliation

God's heart is a heart of reconciliation. Jesus provided a glimpse of God's heart when the Pharisees accused Him of welcoming sinners and eating with them. He shared three stories back to back, recorded in Luke 15, to show God's heart of love for the lost. First, He told of someone who has one hundred sheep and loses one of them. He leaves the ninety-nine to reclaim the one that is lost. If they didn't get that one, Jesus came right back with another: A woman loses one of her ten coins. She turns the house upside-down to find that one lost coin — it is so valuable to her.

If the Pharisees didn't understand the meaning of those two parables, perhaps one closer to home would do the trick. A son takes advantage of his father's generosity and leaves home to squander it on wild and crazy living. When the son finally realizes his error, he returns to dear old dad to confess his wrongdoing and repent. The father reconciles with the son and throws a party in his honor.

Three stories back to back — all to show one thing: God loves the lost and will do whatever it takes to seek and to save them. They are valuable to Him, worth an extraordinary amount effort and patience to retrieve.

Ministers of Reconciliation

Jesus came to seek and to save what was lost – us (Luke 19:10)! He has *compassion* on the lost who are like sheep without a shepherd. He has sought us, drawn us, called us, and reconciled us, and then made us ministers of reconciliation (2 Corinthians 5:11-21). He gave His church the mission of reaching the entire world with the gospel, because God does not want anyone to perish, but everyone to come to repentance (2 Peter 3:9). What does that mean for small groups? Everything!

As His children, formed in His image, we have been given the job of reconciliation. As His children, we are here to seek and save the lost. I love how Wayne McDill put it: "In a world characterized by self-seeking, the Christian is seeking others, not for what they can do for him but for what God will do for them."[1] A person after God's own heart has a compassion for people far away from God and wants to see them reconciled with their Creator and Father!

> *God loves the lost and will do whatever it takes to seek and to save them.*

We are partners, ambassadors, light of the world, in this great mission that Jesus started and then passed on to us. Jesus often referred to Himself as the light of the world (John 1:4-5; 3:19-21; 8:12; 12:46). He also said,

> You *are the light of the world. A city on a hill cannot be hidden. Neither do people light a lamp and put it under a bowl. Instead they put it on its stand, and it gives light to everyone in the house. In the same way, let* your *light shine before men, that they may see your good deeds and praise your Father in heaven. (Matthew 5:14-16; emphasis mine)*

We are now the Light of the World — or at least we are supposed to be. "As the Father has sent me, I am sending you," He told His disciples. In a world of increasing darkness we are the Light, so that anyone who believes in Jesus will not continue to walk in darkness. Small groups are lighthouses in their neighborhoods, workplaces, and schools. They are the places where Christ's commission is carried out.

Reconciliation: the Heart of Small Groups

Do you remember the first time you were invited to a small group? I do. I had visited Centerville Christian Church in Dayton, Ohio and met a few people my age. They invited me to their group; I noticed that some of them were single and others were married, but that didn't matter; they all seemed to have a strong desire to grow in the Lord, and they genuinely cared about each other. Besides that, they were fun to be around!

I especially remember how it felt to be invited. I felt like they wanted me to be part of their group, to be a friend. One of the greatest human needs is the need to feel wanted, the desire to be included in the lives of others. I also felt cared about. They were genuinely concerned about my spiritual life. Unlike some other churches I had visited, I didn't feel like a "spiritual conquest" among these Christians. They cared about me as a person, and I felt like they wanted to be my friends. To me, that made all the difference in the world.

Like the friends from my first group, we have the great privilege of inviting people to our small groups, especially when they do not yet know Jesus as Savior and Lord. But remember, it is God who is doing the calling. In John 12:32, Jesus said He would draw all men to himself. God had already been drawing me to Himself when I first showed up the group. He had used relatives and co-workers, friends, and even an ex-girlfriend's grandmother to move me toward Himself. That small group was sensitive to the Spirit's moving and invited someone to their group whom Jesus was already drawing. I was God's invited guest to their group; they were simply the people who got to extend the invitation!

> We have the great privilege of inviting people to our small groups, especially when they do not yet know Jesus as Savior and Lord.

The key factor is prayer. Prayer puts the power of evangelism where it belongs: in God's hands. Evangelism without prayer has been compared to explosives without a detonator. Prayer without evangelism is said to be like a detonator without explosives.

We are God's partners in redeeming the world. It is a human-divine collaboration. Joe Ellis says, "God's work is accomplished by a combination of human and divine effort. We cannot do it without Him; He has ordained not to do it without us. We depend on each other."[2]

God has given us the responsibility, and the opportunity, to share what He has freely given us. He never leaves us alone in the task. We witness by His power and wisdom. As we seek to bring people into a vertical relationship with the Father, we bring them into a horizontal relationship with others who already have that vertical relationship.

> To go into the world, we must be willing to go onto their turf — to meet unbelievers where they are, not where we expect them to be.

At the church in Indiana where I ministered for several years, we referred to our small groups as "Community Groups." We did this for two important reasons: 1) they were where authentic Christian community took place, and 2) they were the main place for the church reaching into the community.

These small groups were places where friends were made and grown and where the New Testament "one anothers" were lived out. They were environments where intimacy, trust, and accountability grew. They were the body of Christ in action.

They were also a primary way for the church to reach into the community, as each person and group reached its *oikos* — the Greek term meaning household with an applied meaning of a person's or group's web of relationships or sphere of influence.

We wanted to be part of Christ's commission for his church: to go into the world around us and make disciples, baptizing them, assimilating them into Christ's body, and teaching them to obey everything Christ has commanded us. These groups were where people experienced Christ's continuing presence with us.

To go into the world, we must be willing to go onto their turf — to meet unbelievers where they are, not where we expect them to be. I have heard some people proclaim, "But if we strive too hard to reach the world by going where they are, it may result in compromise."

Jesus said it is the sick who need a doctor, not the well (Luke 5:31). He never changed His way of ministering to the downcast because He was afraid of compromising His position. Jesus was a *friend* of the sinners, the society misfits, the hurting, and the people who could ruin his reputation. But He did not enter into their sinful ways. The church needs to follow the model of Christ and be a friend to the very same kind of people, regardless of what others might think.

Jesus compromised nothing. In fact, it is we who compromise the gospel when we sit in our churches, afraid to reach out to the "sinners" in our world. We compromise when we won't go onto their turf. We cannot expect them to come to us at first — we must go where they are, just as Jesus did.

How to Do Group Evangelism: Plant Seeds

Jesus taught that evangelism is very simple:

This is what the kingdom of God is like. A man scatters seed on the ground. Night and day, whether he sleeps or gets up, the seed sprouts and grows, though he does not know how. All by itself the soil produces grain — first the stalk, then the head, then the full kernel in the head. As soon as the grain is ripe, he puts the sickle to it, because the harvest has come. (Mark 4:26-29)

That's it: plant the seed of the gospel! God does the rest. The farmer does not even know what causes the growth. We do know, however, what we need to do to promote that growth. In the case of seed, put it in good ground, water it, fertilize it perhaps, and sit back and watch. Like my kids, all my wife and I need to do is put the right conditions or elements in place and they grow by themselves even though we don't know how.

The apostle Paul restated this fact: "I planted the seed, Apollos watered it, but God made it grow. So neither he who plants nor he who waters is anything, but only God who makes things grow" (1 Corinthians 3:6-7).

> *Evangelism is all about influence.*

Over the years, many churches have made evangelism something difficult, something that takes years to learn, something only for the special few who are gifted, skilled, and learned. They have effectively closed off witnessing to the paid staff and the evangelism committee. In these churches, evangelism happens only on certain nights. Yes, over the years the church has developed some very unbiblical views of evangelism.

Real evangelism is a natural part of the Christian life. As Jim Petersen said, "This kind of evangelism can hardly be called an activity in which one engages on certain occasions. It is *life*. Living itself becomes evangelistic."[3] We may not all have the spiritual gift of evangelism, but we are all called to be witnesses of what Christ has done and is doing in our lives. We should live by the words of Francis of Assisi: "Preach the gospel at all times, and if necessary, use words." When people see that our faith in Jesus means everything to us they will take notice and be drawn to what gives us life.

Evangelism is all about influence. Within our own spheres of influence — *oikos* — we plant the seeds of the good news. As we enter into the world, we have a choice: to be the influenced or to be the influencers. When we live our lives for Christ and choose to be influencers, God uses us in incredible ways.

Christians can also be positive or negative witnesses for God. This is nothing new. Paul wrote to the Jews, "God's name is blasphemed because of you" (Romans 2:24). I like how *The Message* translates this: "It's because of you Jews that the outsiders are down on God."

Can the same be said about some Christians today? Are people "down on God" because of the words and actions of some believers and churches? I'm not just talking about certain TV evangelists who have "fallen." I'm thinking of how people act at work, in their neighborhoods, on their teams, in their schools, and in other places where they have influence.

Neil Cole makes this point emphatically:

I think that the lost of the world will respond well to truth that we embrace wholeheartedly and do not compromise in any way. . . . I have found that lost people who want to be saved respond well to authentic lives willing to admit their need for forgiveness and grace. I have found that those who need their lives changed thrive in a safe place where others are willing to openly confess their own deficiencies. In fact, it is when we hide this authenticity from the world, and pretend to be better than we are, that the world takes offense at our hypocrisy and rejects our message.[4]

Cole's point is so true. The *best* place for people to respond to God's gift is in the environment of an authentic, loving small group. People yearn for something real, something true, and something that will make a real and true difference in their lives. Group leaders have a responsibility to provide such a place and to facilitate that kind of community.

The Leader's Role in Group Evangelism

Authenticity is as important among brothers and sisters in Christ as it is around unbelievers. If small group leaders say that we should all be witnesses, yet do not do so themselves, this hypocrisy teaches people to be disobedient. It gives the message, "I *say* you should share your faith, but I do not really mean it because, as you can see by my actions, I don't really do it."

People in churches have become very accustomed to "Do as I say, not as I do" thinking. When the leaders model that kind of hypocrisy in the group, it turns the group inward and brings about a sickness that is difficult to overcome.

> *The best place for people to respond to God's gift is in the environment of an authentic, loving small group.*

We do not need any more armchair theologians as small group leaders! We do not need people who talk ministry without ever doing it. We need doers of the Word, men and women of action spurred on by God's call on their lives. We desperately need leaders who will model reconciliation and witnessing.

People will respond when they see their leaders actively committed to disciple making. Leaders like this will redefine the norm. Small groups need leaders like this because small groups must become centers of outreach rather than inward cliques. For the most part, the days of lone ranger evangelism are over. Individuals are not usually charged to fulfill the Great Commission by themselves. Evangelism belongs to small groups who team up to use their collective gifts to impact the world around them. The small group shepherd-leader who has God's heart of reconciliation will develop a lifestyle that puts compassion for lost sheep above the distractions in life.

I feel odd saying that you need to spend less time on your computer, watching TV, or reading the latest book, and more time with people, especially lost people. I think what I am trying to communicate is important, or I would not have written this book, but I realize I cannot just write about community and reaching a lost world — I need to *do* it!

I used to be on several Internet discussion lists, where many well-meaning people spent hours at their computers reading and responding to messages about the church. Many of these exchanges became quite heated at times, and I had to wonder if Satan wasn't laughing. On one occasion, two men were going back and forth about "proper" and "improper" methods of evangelism. Others joined in but the discussion centered mainly on these two intelligent men. Finally I had had enough, so I wrote a great email to put the two men in their places. I told them both, and backed it up with relevant Scriptures, that they needed to stop talking about evangelism and actually get out and do it.

Just before I hit the "send" button, I read my own words. I realized that I had become the chief of the hypocrites. Who had I shared the gospel with lately? Had I walked among the people lately and felt compassion for those who are like sheep without a shepherd? The answer was a resounding no. I had become too busy on the discussion lists, reading articles and books about small groups and evangelism, and preparing to write and do workshops to convince other Christians how important lost people are.

All of this flies in the face of the lifestyle we are called to live as Christ's ambassadors. Paul spoke about this when he said,

> *Our gospel came to you not simply with words, but also with power, with the Holy Spirit and with deep conviction. You know how we lived among you for your sake. You became imitators of us and of the Lord; in spite of severe suffering, you welcomed the message with the joy given by the Holy Spirit. (1 Thessalonians 1:5-6)*

Paul's life, like Jesus', was lived among the people for their sake. The simplicity of these two men's lives can be difficult for many of us to replicate today. The pattern of our lives is often marked by perplexity and preoccupation.

Satan is a master of diversion. He keeps us busy with complicated lives so that we never make the impact on our world that we could make, that we are called and authorized to make. He lures us away from the most vital thing, reconciling lost people with their God, with relatively trivial matters — you know what they are in your life!

> *Life may never be simple, but that does not have to stop us from developing relationships and sharing the gospel.*

I was most effective in sharing the gospel at a time when my life was less complicated. We were living in an apartment building, which meant less work to do "around the house." It gave us access to many people who were wandering through life like sheep without a shepherd. Oh how I yearn again for a simplified life!

Life may never be simple, but that does not have to stop us from developing relationships and sharing the gospel. We must allow the Holy Spirit to guide how we spend our time. We must learn to be more strategic, to bring others along as we do ordinary activities, for instance.

The Lifestyle of a Reconciling Leader

A small group leader with a heart of reconciliation is involved in several good habits. Here are some of the things a reconciling group leader does regularly.

Pray.

I discussed prayer at length earlier in this chapter and in the previous chapter. The power for evangelism must come from God, not us.

Begin by praying for the group. Pray that God will use the group to accomplish His purposes and reach lost and wandering sheep. Pray for individuals in the group by name, asking God to make them into fishers of men. Pray for group members' friends who are non-Christians, by name if possible.

Next, meet with your interns and pray with them for the group, for individuals in the group, and for their lost friends. Model a praying lifestyle to them, and include them in the essential ministry of prayer.

Take interns and other potential leaders with you as you visit members and potential members of the group to pray for them. As you visit members, make a point to ask them about people in their spheres of influence *(oikos)* and how you can pray specifically for their needs, especially their spiritual needs.

Finally, make prayer a priority in group meetings. Here are a couple ways to keep evangelistic prayer central.

- Make a prospect list (*The Blessing List* is a great tool available from TOUCH®) of members' friends, co-workers, neighbors, and family members. Hang the list in your meeting room, and discuss the prospects at each meeting, praying for their salvation. If you can get pictures of some of the prospects to tape to the list, all the better!

- Have each group member write down the names of unsaved people in their spheres of influence on a large index card, writing their own name on the other side of the card. Collect all of the cards and place them in the center of the room, then pray for people represented by the cards. Hand the cards back to the members, and instruct them to keep the card in a place (such as their Bibles) where they will remember to pray for these people every day.

- Have members talk with unsaved friends to ask if they can pray for any specific personal needs. They should promise to pray each day for those needs and let their friends know that the small group will pray for them that week. Keep to your promises, and then have the member revisit the person the following week to inquire how God has been answering their prayers.

- Use the "empty chair." Pray each week for the people who will next fill the empty chair in your meeting room. The empty chair has never won anyone to Christ, but it can be used as a reminder to pray for new people and to invite them to the group.

- Do prayer walks in the neighborhood where the group meets.

Go!

Don't get stuck in a "Come to us" mindset. The first verb in the Great Commission is "go"! As a leader, you must set the pace. Like Ralph Neighbour, visit the saloons or other places in your area where unbelievers regularly hang out and seek to minister to people there. Take your intern and other group members with you as you go into the world with the Gospel.

> *Take your intern and other group members with you as you go into the world with the Gospel.*

Both individually and as a group, you have to go where non-Christians are instead of waiting for them to come to you. This will help you break out of the "holy huddle" inclination. Go as a group to festivals, car shows, home shows, shopping malls, anywhere unbelievers gather, and look for opportunities to reach out to people.

Watch.

As I wrote this section, I was sitting in an airport restaurant in Phoenix, Arizona, waiting for my connecting flight. A Middle-Eastern looking businessman sat next to me while I typed. For the first few moments, I continued writing. But then an urging of the Holy Spirit moved me to speak to the man. So I closed my laptop and turned to him. I can't say he crossed the line of faith right there, but I did plant seeds, and we had an interesting conversation in which I was able to share about my faith in God.

As we go through life, we must watch for the opportunities God puts in our path and then "make the most of every opportunity," letting our conversation be always full of grace, seasoned with salt (Colossians 4:5-6).

Serve.

Random, and not-so-random, acts of kindness are great ways to reach out to lost people and show them God's love in a practical way. Handing out cold drinks on a hot day in a park, washing cars for free, and a variety of other deeds are opportunities for the group to go as a team and make a real impact for Christ. See Steve Sjogren's book *Conspiracy of Kindness* or go to http://www.kindness.com for more ideas and information.

Party.

Throw parties, barbecues, game nights, and other social activities regularly; invite people on your prospect list, as well as other non-Christians. Make this a friendship-building opportunity where people are welcomed; Enjoy spending time together, and let them see Christians having fun.

These "Matthew Parties" (named after the dinner party Matthew threw for Jesus, His disciples, and some of Matthew's tax-collecting friends) are great opportunities for your friends to develop relationships with Jesus and His followers. Some churches call these Acquaintance Making Events (AMEs). The purpose of an AME is simple, says Larry Gilbert: "to help develop a three-way relationship between you, an unsaved or unchurched friend, and the members of the group."[5] Other churches call them "Bridge Events" because they are an opportunity to build bridges of relationships. One option is to work with several other groups from your church (or your zone, district, or huddle) and throw the party together.

> *As we rub shoulders with people living in darkness, we are the Light of the world to them.*

These parties are net-fishing or seed-casting events. As we rub shoulders with people living in darkness, we are the Light of the world to them. As we make the most of each opportunity, the Holy Spirit ministers through us into their lives.

Listen.

Before we win the right to share, we must be willing to listen and be genuinely interested in people's stories, interests, ideas, and concerns. Jesus can meet every need an unbeliever has, but we must first try to understand what needs are present, just as Jesus did. A leader who models listening in the small group teaches group members this essential attitude and skill. Listening develops trust and receptivity on the part of the non-Christian. If we do not listen to them, they may never really hear our message!

Speak.

"Always be prepared to give an answer to everyone who asks you to give the reason for the hope that you have. But do this with gentleness and respect" (1 Peter 3:15). When the time comes to speak words of life, speak! But remember, "if anyone speaks, he should do it as one speaking the very words of God" (1 Peter 4:11). Share God's Word with a balance of conviction and compassion. Conviction because the gospel message is the truth and has the power to transform lives. Compassion because that is Jesus' heart toward those who are lost. Sincere love for people can break down the barriers between an unbeliever and Christ. If I share the gospel message with a thousand unbelievers but have not love, I am only a resounding gong or a clanging cymbal. My words might fall on deaf ears, but love never fails!

Wait.

Remember that salvation is a process, and it takes time for people to work through a variety of thoughts, emotions, and decisions of the will. Sometimes numerous obstacles to accepting Christ must be removed just like clearing out trees, rocks, roots, and clay before a field is ready for seeds. Your job may well be to "prepare the way for the Lord" (Matthew 3:3). You may never get to see the harvest itself, but that's not the point. Be faithful with the assignment God gives you. He will take care of the rest in His time, according to His plan.

Team.

All of these practices can be accomplished individually or as a team. Individual Christians should live a witnessing lifestyle, wherever they are, but evangelism works best when teamwork is involved. As every person's individual gifts are utilized, the body of Christ operates as it should. My wife's gift of mercy and her natural ability to build friendships wonderfully complements my gifts of evangelism and leadership. Combine us with other members of our group who have gifts of hospitality, helps, intercession, and shepherding, and we can reach people in a way that none of us can alone.

Train.

Take your intern or another group member with you when you share the gospel. They can help keep distractions to a minimum, but their main objective should be to watch, listen, and learn. Group members need to learn that this is what group life — and Christian life — is all about!

> *Remember that salvation is a process, and it takes time for people to work through a variety of thoughts, emotions, and decisions of the will.*

Celebrate.

Each step a pre-Christian makes toward salvation is a reason to celebrate, but the real festivities begin when the person submits to Jesus as Savior and Lord. Small groups should rejoice fervently when one of their own accepts Jesus as Savior. In our church, the small group leader often baptizes the new believer, and the group stands around the baptistery. It is a ceremony that the rest of the church gets to observe. But for the small group, it is a festive occasion. They had a part in this act of reconciliation between the Father and His newly adopted child. It's time to celebrate!

Of course, it's not enough to make converts. Our mission is to make disciples, baptize them, and teach them to obey Christ's commands, especially His command to make disciples. Such a simple and ingenious plan: Go, and make disciples who will go, and make disciples, who will . . . well, you get the point.

Heart to Heart

1. God's passion is to reconcile lost and hurting people to a relationship with Him. When you examine your own heart, how does your passion for lost people compare to God's? Why?

2. What do you think is the small group's role is reconciling people back to God? How much time and effort should a group put into reaching out to non-Christians? What would a group be willing to change or sacrifice to be more passionate for seeing people come to Christ as Savior?

3. Describe the human-divine collaboration of evangelism. What's God's part? What's our part?

4. Discuss a plan for making your group a natural place for evangelism to happen. What will be the leaders' roles?

Chapter Eight

A Heart for Discipleship

King David had compassion for the people who did not have a relationship with the God of Israel, the one true God. Yet his heart extended beyond the level of compassion. He wrote, "Future generations will be told about the Lord. They will proclaim his righteousness to a people yet unborn" (Psalm 22:30-31).

David's heart saw past his own sphere of influence: the people of Israel under his reign. It stretched to the ends of the earth and even to those yet unborn! That kind of compassion requires much more than personal evangelism; it demands multiplication, replication, reproduction. It is what discipleship is all about.

David's words foreshadow Jesus' to His disciples:

Go and make disciples of all nations, baptizing them in the name of the Father and of the Son and of the Holy Spirit, and teaching them to obey everything I have commanded you. And surely I am with you always, to the very end of the age. (Matthew 28:18-20)

Jesus gave His disciples a mission: to make disciples. Disciples are the "product," but they are also the method or "means of production"! The Great Commission is not just about evangelism, although winning the lost to Christ is certainly a big part of it. It is really about making "fully devoted followers of Jesus Christ" — in other words, disciples who make disciples.

The Law of Multiplication

While I was associate editor at *The Lookout* magazine, a reader sent in a scathing letter disagreeing with an article we had printed about the Great Commission. She argued that Jesus gave the Commission only to His apostles and not to Christians today. The thought is absurd! Jesus would not give instructions, especially instructions this important, that would be impossible to fulfill. Just think about it, it would have been impossible for twelve men, or even one hundred and twenty people, to disciple *all* nations. The genius of Jesus' strategy is that His Commission would be passed from disciple to disciple to disciple, through all generations, until the entire world could be discipled.

Jesus spent most of His time with twelve average men: self-employed businessmen, civil servants, and the like. During the three years He was with them, they were undependable, slow to learn, and self-absorbed. Yet Jesus' plan was simple: to disciple these twelve men and then turn them loose to take the most important message of all time to the entire world. What if they failed?

What was Plan B? There was no other plan! Jesus could have devoted His time to saving masses of people, but He could not have had the kind of intimate relationships with them that He had with His apostles. The genius of his strategy is this: By spending time intensely discipling a few in the setting of community, he equipped them to multiply His message over and over again, all across the earth.

> The genius of Jesus' strategy is that His Commission would be passed from disciple to disciple to disciple, through all generations, until the entire world could be discipled.

Jesus did spend time with the crowds, but He focused on smaller groups, particularly the twelve, and especially the three — Peter, James, and John. After Pentecost, the apostles spent time with the crowds in the temple courts, but they concentrated on house-to-house community in smaller groups.

In years past, the church reached out to the multitudes through rallies, revivals, and crusades. This was the law of addition. It works this way, for example: An evangelist wins one thousand people per day (a rather good harvest!). At the end of one year he has won 365,000 people, and at the end of twenty-five years, he will have won 9,125,000 people to Christ!

As impressive as this number of salvations may seem, the law of addition illustrated here was not the strategy of Jesus or the early church. Why is this? For one thing, in the law of addition, there is little or no attention placed on conserving the harvest, connecting new members to the body, and helping them become healthy, growing disciples who are able to teach others

(Hebrews 5:11 – 6:1). Disciples making disciples is the law of multiplication, which works differently and more slowly — at first. Say a disciple wins and trains one person a year. At the end of one year, there are two disciples. Each of those two disciples wins and trains one person the following year, and so on. At the end of twenty-five years, 33,554,432 disciples will have been won and taught. It would take the evangelist nearly ninety-two years to win that many people to Christ without being able to adequately disciple them. Using the multiplication method as described above, the entire world could be discipled in less than thirty-five years!

Created to Reproduce

Before going much further, we need to understand a fundamental principle: God created us to reproduce ourselves. From the beginning and all throughout Scripture, God has said, "Be fruitful and increase in number" (Genesis 1:28; 9:1, 7; 17:20; 28:3; 35:11; 47:27; 48:4; Exodus 1:7; etc.). Reproducing ourselves is at the heart of who we are; it is part of our genetics. God's purpose is for human beings to be fruitful.

Reproduction is built into *every* human conformation. In a human family, it is natural to bear children, and then for those children to mature and eventually leave home to begin their own families. A human cell does not *decide* whether or not to multiply itself. It just does, or it dies. It is part of its make-up. The same is true of cell groups!

The New Testament often uses the Old Testament concept of fruitfulness and multiplication. John the Baptist warned the crowds who were coming to him to be baptized, "Produce fruit in keeping with repentance. . . . The ax is already at the root of the trees, and every tree that does not produce good fruit will be cut down and thrown into the fire" (Luke 3:8-9). In Jesus' allegory of the vine and the branches, Jesus said we show ourselves to be His disciples by bearing "much fruit" (John 15:8). In other words, disciples are created to reproduce! Those who are connected to the Vine do so automatically (John 15:5).

> *We need to understand a fundamental principle: God created us to reproduce ourselves.*

Paul shared his mental struggle with life and death with the Philippian church. He summarized it saying, "For to me, to live is Christ and to die is gain. If I am to go on living in the body, this will mean fruitful labor for me" (Philippians 1:21-22). In other words, living itself ought to be equivalent to fruitfulness!

God designed His church to reproduce, and we see it do just that in the Book of Acts. Leaders must understand that the power to reproduce is already built into the foundation of the church. We don't need to design human systems or impose outside multiplication strategies; reproductive power is already part of the DNA. All we need to do is learn how to tap into God's power.

This should be as natural as human, animal, or plant reproduction. But we see that as too easy and simple! So we add programs and systems and eventually, we spend so much time running the programs that we no longer reproduce. That's what happened to the Pharisees of Jesus' day, and it happens in many churches today. Let's shift our attention from developing more and better methods to developing more and better people who God will use to bring life.

> *Churches and groups that do not reproduce, die.*

Churches and groups that do not reproduce, die. The good news is that God can resurrect the dead! The Holy Spirit has the power to breathe life into lifeless individuals, groups, and churches. We do not have the power to bring life where there is none, so we must depend on the One who can. Jesus is the resurrection and the life. He came so that we may have life — life to the full. When we depend on Him as Lord of our groups, He will bless us with vitality and fruitfulness.

Real Leadership Multiplies

The business world has come to understand the fact that leadership must replicate itself for an organization to be healthy and grow. Ralph Nader said, "I start with the premise that the function of leadership is to produce more leaders, not more followers." These days, business leaders talk a lot about delegation, mentoring, empowerment, and leadership development.

Believers in the New Testament church seemed to know this instinctively. In churches that are reaping the harvest today, group leaders understand their call to transform group members into group leaders and spawn new groups. They emphasize reproducing or multiplying *leaders*, not just the group. We often talk about multiplying our small group; the problem is that this often stays in the realm of ideas. Also, it is biblically backwards. God's Word teaches us to produce and reproduce *disciples*. When we do that, groups will multiply naturally.

Real leaders multiply. But an important principle applies here: we need to be sure that we are reproducing the right thing! Multiplying weak and feeble believers is dangerous. Jesus spent three years preparing His followers before telling them to go and make disciples. If they had replicated their own lives, the results would have been tragic. But because they reproduced Jesus' life by the power of the Holy Spirit (Acts 1:4-8), the church prospered and continues to bear fruit today. This is why the heart and soul of a small group leader is so important.

God intends for godly disciples to multiply themselves over and over again not only to keep His enterprise "in business," but because it is the most effective way of reaching a world that He wants reconciled to Himself. He has given us a big job to do and has promised His power to carry it out, but there are still problems left for us to diagnose and resolve before moving forward.

Diagnosis: Impotence

I love the description of small groups as "leader breeders." But there is a problem in most small groups and many churches: they are not reproducing — they are impotent. They are not even *excited* about reproducing! What they need is a prescription of Spiritual Viagra®! Here are six contributing factors for groups that are not reproducing:

Wrong Goal

Groups that see fellowship as the primary goal of the meeting will never be leader breeders. Building nurturing, caring community *is* important, but we must see it in one of three ways: (1) the means by which discipleship happens, (2) the environment in which discipleship occurs, or (3) the by-product of discipleship. When new leaders know their mission, to reproduce leadership, they will help grow the kind of church God had in mind from the beginning.

Wrong Focus

Many groups overemphasize Bible study. This might sound harsh, but the purpose of the group is not Bible knowledge, rather it is love for one another (discussed thoroughly in Chapter 5). I feel like I'm constantly struggling just to get people to stop calling our small groups "Bible studies" or "classes." Their verbiage describes their perception of their groups' focus. Groups and classes have been studying the Great Commission for years, but they have not been *doing* it.

No Goals or Focus

Many small groups are more reactive than proactive. They are battered by the waves like the house that the foolish man built on the sand (Matthew 7:24-27).

He was foolish because he had no foresight. The wise man planned. His values (a house that would withstand storms) guided his actions (to build upon rock). A group with no vision, goals, or plans for multiplication will perish (Proverbs 15:22).

Shortsightedness

The excuse most leaders give for not producing new leaders is that no one is ready or that no one wants to start a new group. Too often, the reason for this is that the leader has not done the essential tasks of shepherding, discipling, and empowering the group members. Many of these leaders are simply shortsighted. They look no further than the next meeting. They probably perceive group leadership only as preparing for and facilitating (or teaching) the next lesson.

Many group leaders leave real discipleship to happenstance. If it happens while they do the study, wonderful! Making disciples is the *mission*, so it should never be left to chance.

> *The excuse most leaders give for not producing new leaders is that no one is ready or that no one wants to start a new group.*

Secular Shepherding

Many believers receive more discipling from secular culture then they do from the church. Perhaps television has been their true shepherd and mentor. Those who are taught by television involuntarily fulfill Jesus' words: "Everyone who is fully trained will be like his teacher" (Luke 6:40). That is scary! Many people calling themselves Christians are products of television more than the Word of God. Characters in sitcoms and commercials, news anchors, and MTV performers shape their worldviews more than Jesus. No wonder many of our groups are producing so little — or perhaps rotten — fruit!

The "Hard Act to Follow" Syndrome

Another reproduction stopper in groups is the super-gifted or super-spiritual leader. For example, Larry is one of the best small group leaders in our church. He writes all his own lessons for the Bible study (Word) time of the meeting. His studies are creative, fun, educationally sound, and involvement-oriented. I'm sure most of them are publishable. One day, he came to a striking realization as we talked over lunch. "Maybe the reason I'm not raising up leaders in my group," he said, "is because they figure they could never write the lessons like I do." Like many other "super leaders," Larry had unwittingly set up unrealistic expectations for any potential leaders in his group.

The Remedy

Joel Comiskey reports good news for aspiring group leaders. His research shows that the ability to multiply leadership does not depend on attributes like personality, education, or social status. Even spiritual giftedness does not make a big difference in a leader's ability to produce new leaders. Comiskey says, instead, that group leaders who multiplied their groups spend time with God in prayer for their meeting, their members, and their members' non-Christian friends. They also spend more time interacting with and shepherding the people of their groups. And one final thing: "They fastened their eyes on one goal — reaching a lost world for Jesus through cell multiplication."[1]

All Leaders Must Die!

Reproduction involves a cost. For female salmon and male Black Widow spiders, the cost is death!

Jesus reiterated the great cost of being His disciple:

I tell you the truth, unless a kernel of wheat falls to the ground and dies, it remains only a single seed. But if it dies, it produces many seeds. The man who loves his life will lose it, while the man who hates his life in this world will keep it for eternal life. (John 12:24-25)

There is no multiplication without first dying to self! "Put to death therefore whatever belongs to your earthly nature" (Colossians 3:5). "Count yourselves dead to sin but alive to God in Christ Jesus" (Romans 6:11; see vv. 1-14 for a full discussion of this issue). "A man reaps what he sows. The one who sows to please his sinful nature, from that nature will reap destruction; the one who sows to please the Spirit, from the Spirit will reap eternal life" (Galatians 6:7-8).

Discipleship means sacrifice, but that sacrifice, in the end, bears fruit: "Let us not become weary in doing good, for at the proper time we will reap a harvest if we do not give up" (Galatians 6:9).

The kind of cost Jesus and Paul talk about is complete self-denial, something we find hard to swallow in our culture today. Nonetheless Jesus said, "If anyone would come after me, he must deny himself and take up his cross and follow me. For whoever wants to save his life will lose it, but whoever loses his life for me will find it" (Matthew 16:24-25).

To the people of Jesus' time, taking up a cross was a very serious thing. If you saw a man carrying a cross, it meant he was about to die! Today, a cross has become just a piece of jewelry to many. We often use the term flippantly.

If a garbage bag tears on the way to the curb, well, that's just my cross to bear. I've caught myself saying the same thing about my diabetes: "Well, taking shots and watching my diet the rest of my life is just my cross to bear." But the cross is much more than mere inconvenience! For Jesus, it was the essence of mission. It is the core of self-denial. It is the heart of a sacrificial lifestyle of following Jesus.

This lifestyle is essential to being a disciple: "Any of you who does *not* give up everything he has cannot be my disciple" (Luke 14:33, my emphasis). This means relinquishing any claim I have to run my own life. It means that I view life differently. I'm no longer at the center of things; God is. It means that I say no to self and self-centered living and yes to God and His purposes.

> *For multiplication to occur, the New Testament teaches that we must deny ourselves, die to ourselves, consider it all rubbish, and take the nature of a slave.*

The apostle Paul understood and lived this life: "But whatever was to my profit I now consider loss for the sake of Christ. What is more, I consider everything a loss compared to the surpassing greatness of knowing Christ Jesus my Lord, for whose sake I have lost all things. I consider them rubbish, that I may gain Christ" (Philippians 3:7-8).

I wonder if the reason the gospel message has not flourished in America today is because so many American believers have never even considered the idea of denying themselves. It is so un-American. The cell group church has thrived naturally in many other countries around the world, but in America, it struggles. Why? Because we believe strongly in independence. Independent people often find it difficult to enter into authentic Biblical community because of a lack of interdependence — acting as the Body of Christ.

For multiplication to occur, the New Testament teaches that we must deny ourselves, die to ourselves, consider it all rubbish, and take the nature of a slave. Our culture teaches just the opposite. We have been listening more to culture than God's Word. Therefore, the rulers, authorities, and powers of this dark world win many battles (Ephesians 6:12).

Disciples who want to be leaders after God's own heart must learn to deny themselves and follow Jesus. They must put off instant gratification and put God's kingdom and other people's needs above their own wants. What might that mean in real life? I can only speak for myself; you will need to come up with your own list. Here's mine:

- Less TV
- Less sports on TV
- Less time on pointless discussions that have no eternal value (2 Timothy 2:14)
- More Bible reading
- More prayer, especially for others' needs
- More time alone with God
- More mentoring opportunities
- Choosing "ministry opportunities" more selectively — deciding by God's calling more and vainglory less

What's on your list?

Remain and Go

"One of those days Jesus went out to a mountainside to pray, and spent the night praying to God. When morning came, he called his disciples to him and chose twelve of them, whom he also designated apostles" (Luke 6:12-13).

The definition of a disciple is a follower or student of a teacher. It always implies a relationship. When Jesus first called His disciples, He told them to "come" (Matthew 4:19, for instance).

In 1 Corinthians 7, three times Paul repeats his instructions for a believer to "remain in the situation which he was in when God called him" (1 Corinthians 7:20). This does not mean you can never change locations or situations after you have become a Christian; it simply means "being content in any and every situation" (Philippians 4:12). We need to be able to put down deep roots wherever we are planted in order to make ourselves available to God. We need to remain in a place where we can be discipled. Mostly, we need to remain in Christ, so that we can bear much fruit (John 15:4), remain in His love, and obey His commands (John 15:9-10). Remaining in Christ assures quality control. It guaranties that healthy disciples are being reproduced.

Effective Christians can bear fruit right where they are right now: in their workplaces, in their homes, in their neighborhoods, and among friends they already have. If God moves them to a new place of ministry, they should be ready to move, but in the absence of such a call, they should be content to bear fruit right where they are planted.

Jesus gave the command to "go and make disciples" to every one of His followers. We are commanded to remain and be sent, to come and follow, and to go and make disciples. "Gathering and scattering" is God's strategy for building His church.

Fruit must grow and mature *on* the tree — connected to the Vine. But in time it is designed to fall onto the ground where "it dies and produces many seeds" (John 12:24). Those seeds get planted in the ground and some produce other trees that eventually bear more fruit. This natural cycle of reproduction is God's design for His people, too.

Psalm 1:3 describes a man or woman of God as one who is "like a tree planted by streams of water, which yields its fruit in season and whose leaf does not wither. Whatever he does prospers." A tree has the ability to remain right where it is planted and yet, by its fruit, to go and reproduce itself over and over again.

As God's people, we are a gathering and scattering people. The Old Testament shows Israel as is a nation scattered like seed throughout all the earth. In the New Testament, persecution scattered the believers throughout Judea and Samaria (Acts 8:1) and to the ends of the earth (Acts 1:8). This is by God's design so that the Word of God can be spread and multiplied around the world. "Those who had been scattered preached the word wherever they went" (Acts 8:4).

Until then, we are by nature a scattered people, called to go into the world to gather the lost to God. We are not a "come to us" church, but a "go where they are" church. We are the light of the world!

How to Reproduce

A leader with a desire to reproduce leaders must take several practical steps. I mention them in passing here. Many books and articles in magazines such as *Cell Group Journal*™ have been written that go into these processes in more detail.

1. Plant
You have to plant the seed of the gospel before anything else can happen. As a leader, lead the way and model an evangelistic lifestyle. Use some of the ideas from Chapter 7 to help you raise the evangelistic temperature in the group.

2. Water
Once the seed is in the ground, it must be nurtured. Our job as leaders is to provide the right conditions and nutrients to help it grow and mature. New Christians need more than just group time; they need one-on-one discipleship. Organize more mature members to mentor newer believers. Ralph Neighbour's *Mentoring Another Christian* is a great resource for this step.

3. Cultivate

Every living thing is intended to mature. The role of a leader is to use his or her gifts to "prepare God's people for works of service, so that the body of Christ may be *built up* until we all reach unity in the faith and in the knowledge of the Son of God and become *mature*, attaining to the whole measure of the fullness of Christ. *Then we will no longer be infants . . ."* (Ephesians 4:12-14, my emphasis).

> *Effective Christians can bear fruit right where they are right now: in their workplaces, in their homes, in their neighborhoods, and among friends they already have.*

A leader trains and equips members who have been discipled (mentored) as interns (a.k.a. apprentices or leaders in training). All discipled members have the potential to be future leaders, but they must be brought to maturity and equipped. The best training ground is the small group environment, as the intern follows the leader, learns from him or her, and practices leadership.

Finally, a new leader is produced, and then he or she starts the life cycle all over again. *Voila!* We have reproduction.

The church is one generation away from either (a) worldwide fulfillment of the Great Commission by using the awesome, natural power of multiplication, or (b) worldwide extinction of Christianity if we fail to reproduce ourselves. As small group leaders, the choice and opportunity is ours. But first, *we* must die!

Heart to Heart

1. Real leaders multiply themselves. But in far too many small groups that is not the case. Why?

2. "True disciples who want to be leaders after God's own heart must learn to deny themselves and follow Jesus. That means putting off instant gratification and putting God's kingdom and other people's needs above their own wants." What does that mean in real life to you? What might you need to deny to be a godly leader?

3. What is the next step for reproducing leaders in your group? Prayerfully plan how to make multiplication a core value of the group, and a natural part of the group's life.

Chapter Nine

The Heartbeat of Life: Relationships

In the midst of life-threatening attacks and moments of triumph, conspiracy from within his own family and times of familial peace, moral failures and spiritual breakthroughs, David's heart stayed true to two essentials: an intimate relationship with God and transformational friendships with a few people.

As Saul chased after and threatened to kill David, Saul's son Jonathan remained David's close friend. They encouraged each other, wept together, and loved one another as they loved themselves. They swore a friendship with each other that would last beyond their own lifetime (see 1 Samuel 20:16-17, 41-42; 2 Samuel 9).

When David was victorious in battle, the account says "he sent some of the plunder to the elders of Judah, who were his friends" (1 Samuel 30:26).

When David committed adultery with Bathsheba, the prophet Nathan came to David to bring correction and restoration. Nowhere is Nathan called David's friend, yet his ongoing relationship with David was very strong, from the beginning of David's reign when he wanted to build a house for God's Ark, to the very end, when Nathan anointed Solomon as king. He held David accountable, got in his face when David was wrong, and helped him return to God after he had confessed his sin (2 Samuel 12). David and Bathsheba's even named one of their sons Nathan.

When David's son Absalom conspired to take the crown and forced David to flee the city, David depended on his friend Hushai the Arkite as he fought against his son Absalom's conspiracy. Hushai mourned with David after the conspiracy (2 Samuel 15:30-32) and defended David in front of David's enemies (2 Samuel 15:33-34; 17:7, ff.). He was literally an answer to David's prayer (2 Samuel 15:31). For all this, he is called David's friend (15:37; 16:16-17).

After Absalom's death, it was David's friends, the elders of Judah, who restored him and welcomed him back to Jerusalem as king (2 Samuel 19).

David was deeply connected with people in his life. He was a person after God's own heart, a man who desired meaningful, iron-sharpening-iron relationships.

Designed for Community

God created us in His own image, and as we discussed in Chapter 1, God's character includes the fact that He is relational. Before creation, community existed in the Godhead: Three in One.[1]

God enjoys deep, strong, intimate fellowship with His children. He desires communion with us; He designed us to live in authentic community with each other. "It is not good for the man to be alone" (Genesis 2:18). God even ordained that the first two individuals would become "one flesh" (Genesis 2:24). That's community!

> *The heartbeat of the Christian life is relationships: communion with God and community with others.*

The heartbeat of the Christian life is relationships: communion with God and community with others (Matthew 22:37-40). And that, of course, is the heart and soul of the godly small group leader and the transformational small group. It is in authentic community that people find real hope in the midst of pain, loss, loneliness, depression, and sin in our lives. God gave us the gift of community to meet our needs. The real need of our culture is to meaningfully connect with a few other people. When we do, we are able to change, to grow, and to heal.

Entering Community

It is important to understand that we do not — and cannot — *create* authentic community. It already exists in Christ! He has made it possible for us to be reconnected to God and to each other.

Community exists for Christians, but we must enter into it. That is why Jesus prayed for our unity in John 17, "that they may be one as we are one" (John 17:11). Jesus' prayer was for us to be connected with the same oneness that existed in God before the foundations of the world were set in place!

Sin has separated us from communion with God (Genesis 3:8) and from oneness with one another. It causes us to look at one another differently — with judgment rather than grace, with shame instead of transparency (Genesis 3:7).

Jesus broke the cycle of sin, allowing us to enter into communion with God and community with one another once again. When we enter into and experience this community, it changes our world: "May they be brought to complete unity to let the world know that you sent me and have loved them even as you have loved me" (John 17:23).

> *The small group leader's role is not to create community but to prayerfully facilitate the group into entering into it.*

Jesus' prayer for community was extended not only to His disciples, but also to you and me (John 17:20-26). Therefore, this kind of oneness is possible in and through our small groups. Jesus has provided everything needed for our groups to enter into it: "I have given them the glory that you gave me, that they may be one as we are one" (John 17:22). The small group leader's role is not to create community but to prayerfully facilitate the group into entering into it.

To do that, the leader must lead the way, not only by convening a weekly meeting, but also by getting together with group members between meetings for breakfasts or lunches, by personal visits, telephone calls, encouragement notes, or email, and just "hanging out" together.

A while ago, the apprentice of one of our strongest small groups in my church stopped by my office to tell me how great things are going in his group. The fascinating thing is that he did not say a word about how great their Bible study times are or how great their leader is. He told me with lots of excitement about a fishing trip the group just returned from. He shared how the group is growing and how friendships are being built. This group has done an excellent job of 24-7 ministry to one another.

In his *The Key Is the Coach* seminar for TOUCH®, Jay Firebaugh encourages leaders to have a "1-2-3 plan" for connecting with members between meetings:

1) social visit with a group member
2) meetings (the weekly group meeting and a training meeting with their apprentice – although this meeting could be in the form of a phone call)
3) phone calls or notes to members of the group

This is a practical plan for leaders to develop authentic community, but there are still obstacles to overcome as we seek to enter into it.

Roadblocks to Community

Authentic, powerful, transformational community is available to all Christians; Jesus has made it available to us by God's grace. But there are many roadblocks along the way:

Misdiagnosis

Separation has destroyed community. It is a spiritual problem that only God can fix. Unfortunately, our society has misdiagnosed spiritual sickness as psychological disorder. This is the major contention of Dr. Larry Crabb, a licensed psychotherapist for more than a quarter century and author of popular Christian counseling textbooks.

A number of professionals in the counseling field have disagreed vehemently with Dr. Crabb, but I believe his views are right on the mark. Here is a brief sampling of his comments:

- "Beneath what our culture calls psychological disorder is a soul crying out for what only community can provide."
- "Damaged psyches aren't the problem. The problem beneath our struggles is a disconnected soul. . . . Rather than fixing psyches or scolding sinners, we must provide nourishment for the disconnected soul that only a community of connected people can offer."
- "I believe that the root of all non-medical human struggle is really a spiritual problem, a disconnection from God that creates a disconnection from oneself and from others."[2]

Our misdiagnosis has had a detrimental effect on community. When people, even Christians, face life difficulties, they often turn to professional therapists rather than biblical community. Therapy does not really heal the deep pain that only God can heal through community as He has designed it.

Independence

In North America, we value our independence and self-assurance with a passion. The Declaration of Independence is a guiding principle as much as an historical document. Personal rights, personal choice, and even a personal relationship with Christ are our buzz words. We are a society of self-awareness, self-actualization, self-image, self-improvement, self-indulgence, and ultimately, self-centeredness. I love the story about a guy who goes into a bookstore and asks the cashier to point him toward the self-help section. "Wouldn't that defeat the purpose?" she responds.

A small group does not necessarily equal community. In our culture especially, many small groups meet every week and never experience authentic, life-changing community. Many people look to join a group not for what they can add to the group, but for what they can get out of it for their own needs. In fact, many churches promote groups for what the individual can receive, which develops the consumer mindset that is already so prevalent in our society.

In *The Safest Place on Earth*, Larry Crabb describes relationships that people often mistake for authentic community. None of these are spiritual community, however:

> In our culture, many small groups meet every week and never experience authentic, life-changing community.

Congenial Relationships are those in which we stay at a safe distance to avert any kind of conflict. Crabb calls it "defensive civility." Congeniality, however, does not alleviate conflict; it simply hides it.

In *Cooperative Relationships* we work together on projects, even important ones, in surface-level relationships that really only serve our own need for value and prestige. Many church boards function in cooperative relationships (if that!). In cooperative relationships, the task or "business of the group" is more important than people.

In *Consoling Relationships* the highest priority is to make each other feel good about ourselves. Crabb says it almost too poignantly: "Pastors [as well as small group leaders] sometimes say what the itching ears of their congregations [groups] want to hear. Prostitutes do whatever their clients desire. There really isn't much difference." Jesus' relationship with His disciples was hardly consoling. He did not have consolation in mind when He called Peter "Satan"!

Exclusive Relationships are a type of unspiritual community that Dr. Crabb includes with Consoling Relationships, but I believe they are different enough to warrant a separate category. In exclusive relationships we form an inner ring of "community" that is special because it excludes others. These kinds of groups are what Jim Petersen calls "bounded sets." We define the group with boundaries to determine who is in and who is out based on parameters such as appearance, background, age, social class, stands on certain social issues and theological positions, and many more. All these are meant to exclude people, which break down any chance for Trinity-like community.

In *Counseling Relationships*, we analyze underlying causes for problems and work with psychological dynamics to help "fix" someone. This happens in a counselor's office, and far too often in small groups as well. Crabb says that in biblical language it is little more than "rearranging or socializing the flesh." These relationships are not empowered by the Spirit and do not move a person toward maturity in Christ. They are a poor substitute for real community.

Conforming Relationships are those in which individuals feel they must measure up to certain standards. The assumption is that we must earn our ongoing relationship with Christ, even if our initial salvation was by grace. The purpose in such a group is to use the Bible to measure your spiritual and moral areas of weakness and get you to either conform to the group's standards or beat you over the head with it. There is no room for human failure or God's grace. Holiness becomes a straightjacket or yoke imposed by the group rather than what it really is: a gift of God's grace (Romans 6:22; Ephesians 4:22-24).[3]

Crabb concludes this section by sharing the real thing, what he hopes to see develop in place of inauthentic, unspiritual "community":

> My burden is to see spiritual communities develop, where spiritual friends and spiritual directors [small group leaders] *connect* with people. I long to see communities where people feel *safe* enough to be broken. Where a *vision* of what the Spirit wants to do in people's lives sustains them, even when they are far from it. Where *wisdom* from God sees what the Spirit is right now doing and what is getting in His way. Where the literal life of Christ pours out of one to energize that life in another, offering His divine *touch*.[4]

You have an awesome privilege and responsibility to facilitate the group in entering into community where people feel safe enough to be broken — that is, they can be who they really are, without masks, and know they will be accepted for who they are. *You* have the God-given opportunity to allow the Holy Spirit to work through people in the group to touch and heal one another. *You* have the opportunity to build a context where Christ's life can be poured out from the strong to the weak. God wants to use you, leader, to facilitate the pouring out of His blessings upon people in the group. And He will use *all* of you to do that.

Meeting-Mindedness

Conducting a meeting is easy. Building relationships with people is more work, but lots more fun! It's what authentic, biblically functioning small groups are all about.

> *You have an awesome privilege and responsibility to facilitate the group in entering into community where people feel safe enough to be broken.*

In their longing to create community, some leaders confuse the development of small group dynamic skills, such as the study of body language or the skillful asking of questions, with the building of true community. One danger in small group leadership is paying so much attention to group dynamics that community is actually hindered. This happens when leaders become almost mechanical in their "presentation." Their focus turns to "running a great meeting" rather than building community. It is "performance-oriented" rather than "relationship-focused."

Another danger is overemphasizing the meeting time, as if community is built into an hour and a half once a week. I find many leaders think that the meeting and community are the same thing. This fallacy devitalizes many groups.

The early church seemed to come to community naturally. In Acts 2:42-27, one of the key community passages in the Bible, we read that "*every day* they continued to meet together" (Acts 2:46). And the result was that "the Lord added to their number *daily* those who were being saved" (Acts 2:47; cf. 16:5). The Hebrew Christians were also reminded to "encourage one another *daily*, as long as it is called Today" (Acts 3:13). And so "all the believers were one in heart and mind" (Acts 4:32).

Fruit-bearing small groups are more than a meeting and more than a Bible study. They are spiritual families who really care for one another and look to after one another's interests. I've noticed that groups that are focused on a weekly meeting are usually stagnant and stale. Groups that see themselves as spiritual families love one another, flourish, grow, and multiply themselves.

> *Groups that see themselves as spiritual families love one another, flourish, grow, and multiply themselves.*

Monophobia

The fear of being alone (monophobia) often draws people to a group. Entire groups may consist of monophobiacs. But this does not lead to community at all. Just the opposite in fact — it ultimately leads to isolation. Dietrich Bonhoeffer makes a fascinating and accurate point:

> Christian community is not a spiritual sanatorium. The person who comes into a fellowship because he is running away from himself is misusing it for the sake of diversion, no matter how spiritual this diversion may appear. He is really not seeking community at all, but only distraction which will allow him to forget his loneliness for a brief time, the very alienation that creates the deadly isolation of man.[5]

Bonhoeffer goes on to say that people who cannot be alone should beware of community. They could harm themselves as well as the community because they are using the group to satisfy only their own needs. Unfettered, this leads to unhealthy inward focus in the group. Solitude was a normal activity for Jesus. He got away from the crowds to pray often, especially right before major events in His ministry. We also need regular times alone with God in prayer, as well as extended times of solitude to help us get away from the rush of the world.

Solitude is not the opposite of community. They actually form a symbiotic relationship. Solitude by members of the community makes that community stronger. On the other side, time spent in community provides the encouragement, support, and accountability that individuals need in order to spend time in solitude. Bonhoeffer says, "Each by itself has profound pitfalls and perils. One who wants fellowship without solitude plunges into the void of words and feelings, and one who seeks solitude without fellowship perishes in the abyss of vanity, self-infatuation, and despair."[6]

Masks

Many believers attend church services and group gatherings wearing masks to conceal their sinfulness from themselves and the rest of the group. The church is the one place where we should be able to admit our imperfections. "All are sinners," after all! A hidden sinful lifestyle poisons a person from within. Unexpressed sin holds the person in bondage to it.

Confession is the key to removing masks. The idea of *confession* makes some people uncomfortable. Confession of sin is not an option in the Christian life, it is a necessity: "Confess your sins to each other and pray for each other so that you may be healed" (James 5:16). Confession is an integral part of community life; along with genuine repentance and prayer, it helps bring healing to the individual and the community.

The best setting for learning about and eventually practicing Christian confession is the small group. People are more likely to confess their sins among just a few people whom they trust, who can hold them accountable, and who can be held accountable. This isn't going to happen in your first meeting, and maybe not even in your twenty-first. Accountability and trust, the prerequisites to confession, take time.

Bonhoeffer's statements about confession and community are priceless:

He who is alone in his sin is utterly alone. . . . The final break-through to fellowship does not occur, because, though they have fellowship with one another as believers and as devout people, they do not have fellowship as the undevout, as sinners. The pious fellowship allows no one to be a sinner. So everyone must conceal his sin from himself and from the fellowship. We dare not be sinners. Many Christians are unthinkably horrified when a real sinner is suddenly discovered among the righteous. So we remain alone with our sin, living in lies and hypocrisy. The fact is that we *are* sinners! . . .

In confession the break-through to community takes place. Sin demands to have a man by himself. It withdraws him from the community. The more isolated a person is, the more destructive will be the power of sin over him, and the more deeply he becomes involved in it, the more disastrous is his isolation. . . .

The expressed, acknowledged sin has lost all its power. . . . He can confess his sin and in this very act find fellowship for the first time.[7]

Confession is the missing ingredient in many small groups. The lack of it explains why authentic community does not exists in many groups. It explains why many people who are in good, strong small groups still struggle with ongoing sin, why many leaders are caught in inappropriate affairs, why there is often such a lack of transformation happening in people's lives even though they meet weekly in "community." Bonhoeffer says, "confession is conversion" and "confession is discipleship."

> *The church is the one place where we should be able to admit our imperfections.*

With these things in mind, here are five things you can do to make confession a natural part of your small group.

1. *Know one another.* Community building is an essential part of your meeting. Icebreaker questions and time spent together before and after the "official" meeting time help. People become friends as they begin spending time socially together outside meeting times as well. As they get to know each other, they will be more comfortable with one another. Then they will begin to trust one another.

2. *Be transparent.* Usually the leader needs to open up his or her life before other group members will do the same. When you take off your mask, others will be encouraged to take off theirs. Transparency about little things at first will enable people to be open about bigger things later.

3. *Be confidential.* Group members won't share personal struggles and areas of sin if they think they might be blabbed outside the group. Be sure that everyone knows that things shared in the group stay in the group. Remind them of this especially when a deep concern is expressed.

4. *Carry one another's burdens.* People will open up more when they are sure you really care about them. Leader, be ready to help in times of physical, emotional, and spiritual need. People will respond by sharing their struggles with you.

5. *Hold each other accountable.* Accountability to others is a tough discipline. But we need each other. At first, you can hold one another

accountable for being on time to meetings, then for disciplines such as personal prayer and Bible study, and then, as trust is built, for issues that deal with sin. Remember that accountability must flow from the person being held accountable and never the other way around. In other words, individuals must first ask others to hold them accountable in some area. Forcing accountability on others leads to legalism and cultic behavior. Accountability flows out of loving friendship.

Community Is the Context

Earlier, I discussed several dangers we face as we build community in small groups. There is one more danger to discuss, the notion that the group exists to develop strong, intimate relationships. The commission given to the church is to "make disciples." That is the goal of every small group as well. Community, then, is only the context or environment in which disciples are made.

Remember high school biology? In my school at least, we got to grow organisms in little round vessels called petri dishes. In the bottom of these dishes was a gooey substance that provided the environment and nutrients for growth to occur. Small groups are like petri dishes. They contain the culture or community in which disciples grow.

Discipleship — spiritual transformation — includes at least five essential components:

> *Community is only the context or environment in which disciples are made.*

- *Agent:* The Holy Spirit. Spiritual transformation is a supernatural process. (1 Peter 1:2; Gal. 5:22-25).
- *Goal:* Christlikeness. The goal is not just behavior modification (stop one set of practices to adopt another). We are transformed into new creatures in Christ, a complete change in our values (2 Corinthians 3:18).
- *Means:* The renewing of our minds (Romans 12:2).
- *Context:* Authentic Community. Real transformation happens in the midst of authentic Christian community where the "one another" passages of the New Testament are lived out.
- *Time Frame:* Lifetime Process. Transformation takes a lifetime, but we must start where we are (Philippians 3:12-15).

Discipleship happens naturally in the proper environment: small groups where people live together in authentic, transformational community. The role of the leader is to provide a place for the Holy Spirit to work in the lives of people, to point people toward the goal of Christlikeness.

Communion with God and community with one another: These are God's heart for us, and they are the heartbeat of the Christian life.

Heart to Heart

1. On a day-to-day, week-to-week basis, what practical things can you as a leader do to help people enter into real, dynamic community?

2. What roadblocks to community have you seen or experienced in your group(s)? How did these roadblocks come about? What can be done now to break through these barriers to community?

3. How can confession lead to stronger community and changed lives?

4. Life transformation happens best in the context of authentic community. Why? What first steps can you take to transform your group into a group where lives are regularly being transformed?

Chapter Ten

Heart Attack!

Like David, my desire is to be a person after God's own heart. I want to be in communion with Him every minute of every day; I want to be in authentic, transformational community with other Christians; and I want to be in redeeming relationships with those He is still seeking.

As a small group leader, I desire to see communities where people are communing together with God, seeking His awesome transforming power in their midst and through their lives; I want to see people connecting as true friends who look not only to their own interests, but also the interests of others. I want to see people growing together toward Christlikeness and reaching out as teams to their friends and families and co-workers and neighbors with the life-changing message of the gospel; I want to see group members maturing in their faith and leadership and desiring to reach out beyond themselves through new groups.

> *I believe that multiplying leaders after God's own heart is the way of winning the world to Christ.*

I believe that multiplying leaders after God's own heart is *the* way of winning the world to Christ. *Skilled* leaders won't do it with their abilities. *Charismatic* leaders can't do it on their own. *Intellectual* leaders can't depend on their learning to do it; knowledge just puffs up. None of the *outward* leadership attributes will do it. Remember King Saul?

God is looking for men and women, young and old, after His own heart. Those are the kinds of leaders He will use to bring the world to Himself. God wants people who will throw their lives into following Him and serving Him. First, however, we must count the cost, because it is great. But it is miniscule as compared to the prize. In the end, it will all be worth all the *personal* sacrifice. Community is worth any cost — for Jesus it was worth dying for. His death brought reconciliation between His Father and us and between all of us.

Community is worth death for you and me — starting with death to self. In fact, without death to self, community will never happen. Without death to self, our small groups will be nothing more than assemblies of independent, egocentric individuals who use the group only to meet their own needs. Without death to self, we will never fulfill God's purpose for His world and Christ's commission for His church — we will not have the compassion to want to see the lost saved. In real, transformational community, ego dies. When that happens, new life emerges. Multiplication starts. God is glorified.

> *Without death to self, our small groups will be nothing more than assemblies of independent, egocentric individuals who use the group only to meet their own needs.*

What we need is a "heart attack"! A spiritual battle in which we must arm ourselves with spiritual weapons, not physical ones. Then we will be "strong in the Lord, and in his mighty power" (Ephesians 6:10-18). We will be like David, the "man after God's own heart" who faced the opposition not with sword and spear and javelin, but "in the name of the Lord Almighty" (1 Samuel 17:45).

When God looks for leaders, He looks at our hearts. When He looks at my heart, I want Him to see one yielded to Him, one beating in time with His own, one pounding for Him and His plan. I want to be a person after God's own heart.

What does God see when He looks at your heart? Is it beating more for the things of this world or for God and His will? Do you love Him with all your heart, soul, mind, and strength? Are you thirsting for God? Have you surrendered your dreams and desires for His?

Are you willing to let God form His heart in you? Are you ready to make yourself available for His purposes? If you have answered yes to these questions, you are not a mere man or woman; you are a child of God, and as such you have supernatural power to do the extraordinary works of God that He is calling you to do.

Now you have a decision to make: to keep leading the way you always have or to change the way you are leading; to be a servant rather than a supervisor perhaps; to be a shepherd rather than a teacher; to be a mentor and multiplier rather than a manager and maintainer. If you are willing to allow God to transform you, then you will be His man or woman and He will work through you. When you decide to follow God all the way, regardless of the cost, get ready! You are in for an exciting life . . . life to the full!

God is still searching for leaders, and He is looking for more people like David, men and women after His own heart. I hope when He looks at your heart, He will see a reflection of His own and say, "You are the one! You are a person after my heart. Now come and serve in My kingdom" That is His call to you and His plan for your life.

Heart to Heart

1. This final chapter asks some challenging questions:
   - What does God see when He looks at your heart? Is it beating more for the things of this world or for God and His will?
   - Do you love God with all your heart, soul, mind, and strength?
   - Are you thirsting for God?
   - Have you surrendered your dreams and desires for His?
   - Are you willing to let God form His heart in you?
   - Are you ready to make yourself available for His purposes?

   How did you respond to these questions? How do you feel about being a leader after God's own heart?

2. What will it take for you to remain a godly leader? What do you need from others? Support? Equipping? Encouragement? Prayer? Accountability?

3. Leaders need transformational community too. To whom do you have accountability and a place to confess your sins? If you do not have this yet, what steps will you take?

End Notes

Chapter 1

[1] J. Oswald Sanders, *Enjoying Intimacy with God* (Chicago: Moody Press, 1980), 12.

[2] Larry Crabb, *Connecting: Healing for Ourselves and Our Relationships — A Radical New Vision* (Nashville: Word Publishing, 1999), 158.

[3] Crabb, *Connecting*, 15.

[4] Crabb, *Connecting*, 19.

[5] Joe Ellis, *The Church on Purpose: Keys to Effective Church Leadership* (Cincinnati: Standard Publishing, 1982, 1991), 30.

Chapter 2

[1] This was a line from the Greek comedy *Thais*, which Paul quoted in 1 Corinthians 15:33.

[2] List taken from text of *Leadership by the Book*, pp. 42-43.

[3] Crabb, *Connecting*, 32.

[4] Crabb, *Connecting*, 32.

[5] Bill Hull, *The Disciple Making Pastor* (Grand Rapids, MI: Fleming H. Revell, 1988), 81.

[6] See John 5:17, 19, 30, 36; 6:38, 44, 65; 7:6, 16-18, 28; 8:28, 29, 42, 50, 54; 10:18, 29, 37; 12:49, 50; 14:10, 24, 31. Jesus clearly saw the need to reiterate the idea to His disciples that He depended totally on the Father in His ministry.

[7] Neil Cole, *Cultivating a Life for God: Multiplying Disciples Through Life Transformation Groups* (Carol Stream, Illinois: ChurchSmart Resources, 1999), 4.

Chapter 3

[1] "In his heart a man plans his course, but the Lord determines his steps" (Proverbs 16:9). "Many are the plans in a man's heart, but it is the Lord's purpose that prevails" (Proverbs 19:21). "'Woe to the obstinate children,' declares the Lord, 'to those who carry out plans that are not mine'" (Isaiah 30:1).

[2] Jim Cymbala, *Fresh Wind, Fresh Fire* (Grand Rapids, MI: Zondervan Publishing House, 1997), 148.

[3] Henry T. Blackaby & Claude V. King, *Experiencing God: How to Live the Full Adventure of Knowing and Doing the Will of God* (Nashville: Broadman & Holman Publishers, 1994), 143.

Chapter 4

[1] Gordon MacDonald, *Ordering Your Private World* (Anniversary Edition) (Nashville: Thomas Nelson Publishers, 1984, 85), 52.

[2] The following graphics were adapted from http://www.greatcom.org/spirit/english.

Chapter 5

[1] Cymbala, 143.

[2] Our small group ministry assistant and I created these values using the words in parentheses as

headings at first. Then we realized that four of our five values are similar to TOUCH's® four dynamics of a healthy cell (from their Upward, Inward, Outward, Forward Workshop). We decided to adopt TOUCH's® labels, adding one more, "Onward." TOUCH® uses the one term, "Forward," to describe what we have broken into two separate values, "Forward" and "Onward," giving additional emphasis to each one. By the way, Upward, Inward, Outward, Forward is a dynamic workshop!

Chapter 6

[1] Throughout John's Gospel, we see Jesus stating His complete dependence on God. Here are just a few examples: "The Son can do nothing by himself; he can do only what he sees his Father doing, because whatever the Father does the Son also does" (John 5:19). "For I have come down from heaven not to do my will but to do the will of Him who sent me" (6:38). "My teaching is not my own. It comes down from Him who sent me" (7:16). "I do nothing on my own, but speak just what the Father has taught me" (8:28).

[2] Karen Hurston, "The Small Groups Behind the World's Largest Church," *Strategies for Today's Leader*, Spring 1999, 16.

[3] Hurston, 16-17.

[4] Joel Comiskey, *Reap the Harvest: How a Small-Group System Can Grow Your Church* (Houston: TOUCH® Publications, 1999), 47-48.

Chapter 7

[1] Wayne McDill, *Making Friends for Christ* (Nashville: Broadman Press, 1979), 23.

[2] Joe S. Ellis, *The Church on Target: Achieving Your Congregation's Highest Potential* (Cincinnati: Standard Publishing, 1986), 34.

[3] Jim Petersen, *Living Proof* (Colorado Springs: NavPress, 1989, Fourth Printing, 1991), 120.

[4] Cole, 97.

[5] Larry Gilbert, "Will AMEs and RSAs Help You Reach People for Christ?" *Strategies for Today's Leader*, Spring 1999, 5.

Chapter 8

[1] Joel Comiskey, "Born to Multiply: Reaching a Lost World Through Small Groups," *Strategies for Today's Leader*, Spring 1999, 12.

Chapter 9

[1] Gilbert Bilezikian provides theological elucidation: "Community finds its essence and definition deep within the being of God. Oneness is primarily a divine mode of being that pertains to God's own existence, independently from and prior to any of his works of creation. Whatever community exists as a result of God's creation, it is only a reflection of an eternal reality that is intrinsic to the being of God. Because God is eternally one, when he created in his image, he created oneness" (Gilbert Bilezikian, *Community 101: Reclaiming the Church as a Community of Oneness* [Grand Rapids, Michigan: Zondervan Publishing House, 1997], 16).

[2] The first three statements are from *Connecting*, pp. xvi, xvii. Statement four is from *Connecting*, p. xii. Statement five is from *The Safest Place on Earth*, 47.

[3] Crabb, *Safest Place*, 53-56.

[4] Crabb, *Safest Place*, 56.

[5] Bonhoeffer, 76-77.

[6] Bonhoeffer, 78.

[7] Bonhoeffer, 110-113.